Six Famous Sons
of
Killyleagh

D1464619

Clive Scoular

Published in 2006 by
Clive Scoular
Killyleagh
County Down

© Clive Scoular 2006

ISBN 0-9539601-5-3
ISBN 978-0-9539601-5-6

The author gratefully acknowledges the help given unstintingly by his partner, Thomas Johnston, on the book's layout and design.

Photograph Acknowledgements

The author wishes to thank the following for the use of photographs: Killyleagh Parish Church, First Killyleagh Presbyterian Church, Mr Terry Cochrane and Mr and Mrs Clifford Healy.

Printed in Northern Ireland by
W & G Baird Limited

For the people of Killyleagh

— citizens of distinction

Contents

Introduction

When I first came to live outside Killyleagh almost forty years ago, it did not take me long to realise what a special place it was. Overlooked as it is by its fabulous castle, the village stands proudly on the shores of lovely Strangford Lough. Few of Killyleagh's residents probably appreciate its real importance. With its Royal Charter of 400 years ago and its long list of notable former citizens, Killyleagh has been, in the past, one of Ireland's most prominent locations.

Nowadays, however, outsiders would not consider Killyleagh to be anything other than a mid-way point between Downpatrick and Comber. But hidden behind its present day anonymity lie the stories of famous sons, past and present, whose contribution to the world stage, as well as the local one, has been more than noteworthy.

When asked when I was going to write about Killyleagh's famous sons, I was for some time reluctant to undertake the task. There were, for such a small village, many such people. One major difficulty, of course, in writing such a book is the possibility of being accused of forgetting this person and that. I decided, therefore, to follow my own instincts and have chosen just six of Killyleagh's famous sons.

Most of those whom I have selected did not, of course, live in Killyleagh all their lives. In fact none of them did, but each in his own way has helped put Killyleagh on the map once more. In choosing Hans Sloane, Edward Hincks, Henry Blackwood, Henry Cooke, Terry Cochrane and David Healy, I deliberately selected those whose names are only vaguely known to the local people as well as some whose names are presently household ones. Each of those chosen left Killyleagh or arrived in Killyleagh at different parts of their lives but made a definite contribution to society, both in Ireland and further afield.

Hans Sloane lived his first almost twenty years in Killyleagh; Edward Hincks spent his last 41 years here; Henry Blackwood is only reputed to have been born in the castle but he did spend some of his early years here; Henry Cooke was minister here for just eleven years but during this time wrote his name in large letters in Presbyterian history; and the two footballers, Terry Cochrane and David Healy, although having made their names playing for Northern Ireland, have retained their family links in the village.

Many others who have written their names in the chronicles of the history of Killyleagh have come from all the traditions. The Rowan Hamiltons, whose extensive history has partly been documented in the Dufferin papers, continue to give to Killyleagh their own brand of dignity. The football hero of the 1920s, Hugh Henry Davey, left his indelible mark on Ireland's football history. There have been many others who were proud to have kept the name of Killyleagh well to the forefront.

I dedicate this book to the worthy people of Killyleagh itself. When I came here originally I was given nothing but the greatest help and encouragement when I ran the Scout Troop at the Parish Church. These people are amongst the best natured and open-minded I have ever met. I count it a privilege to name many of them as my friends. Their homes were always open to me. Make a friend in Killyleagh and you have made a friend for life.

As ever I am greatly indebted for all the work of preparation for the book to my partner, Thomas Johnston, without whose assistance I could never have completed it. To Terry Cochrane and David Healy and their families and to countless other people who have helped me in my research, I also want to say a heartfelt thank you.

I trust that by reading this book the people of Killyleagh will once again realise what an important place they live in. They can be rightly proud of their village. Let no one ask what Killyleagh has done for the world – let them look around and they will see.

Clive Scoular
Killyleagh, 2006

Sir Hans Sloane

1.
Early Days by the Lough Shore

There was born on 16 April 1660 arguably Killyleagh's most famous son – Hans Sloane. Nearly four centuries have passed since this notable event which has continued to keep the little county Down village's name to the forefront of interest not only in Ireland but throughout the entire British Isles. Hans Sloane was a truly great man whose legacy to the sciences is almost certainly unequalled.

His birth took place in a modest two storied thatched house on Frederick Street. The dwelling had been built in 1637 and, in 1880, substantially rebuilt. Sadly and scandalously the house was demolished in 1970 to make way for commonplace late twentieth century council houses. Why the birthplace of county Down's leading son was not preserved is a great shame.

Hans was the youngest child of Alexander and Sarah (nee Hicks) Sloane. All of their seven children were sons born one year after each other until Hans' birth in 1660. Only three of the boys survived – James, born in 1655, William, born in 1658 and Hans. Their four other sons died in infancy. When we read of children who 'died in infancy' in the seventeenth century we forget the awful trauma for parents, and particularly for the mothers, of such children. They died from straightforward illnesses which today are quickly cured. Whilst the Sloanes would have been cheered by the lives of their three surviving sons, they would have deeply mourned for Alexander, Henry, John and Robert, who all failed to reach their first birthdays. Little funeral processions to church graveyards were all too common in those days. Life was very much more precarious, but nonetheless precious.

Alexander was a Presbyterian whose family – possibly his own father – had come over from Scotland along with the Hamiltons who soon found both favour and land in county Down. The Sloanes were also people of importance, though not of the gentry classes themselves. Alexander was a land agent for

Sloane's childhood home in Frederick Street

James Hamilton, 2nd Viscount Claneboye. Land agents were powerful men who acted in the absence of the landlords. They were people to be greatly respected, if not actually feared. Thus was Alexander Sloane a stalwart of Killyleagh, or White's Castle as the village was called around that time. He died in 1666 when Hans was just 6 years old.

It would have been a blow to the boy and his two brothers. In 1671 Sarah Sloane remarried and moved away from Killyleagh. Hans and his brothers remained although James, the eldest boy, was just 16 years old. He held the family together until, in due course of time, all three young men moved away to live in England.

Little of Hans' young life is chronicled although we do know that Killyleagh was then a centre of culture and education. We do know that the young Hans did attend one of the church schools in the village. He was brought up as a Presbyterian but, like many of his faith, he was baptised in the Church of Ireland. The rector in St John's church was the Reverend William Richardson who was a clever scholar of his day and generation. But he also had attracted some notoriety. His bishop, the scholarly Dr Jeremy Taylor, had to take action against Richardson by deposing him for non-conformity. One can only imagine what sort of anti-establishment heresy the good rector was preaching, although Presbyterian and Church of Ireland clergy, at that time, often shared churches and pulpits.

Presumably there were tongues wagging in Killyleagh and a certain amount of unease amongst the parishioners. However they soon had a replacement in the Reverend Robert Maxwell. The arrival of Mr Maxwell pleased not only his parishioners but also the budding scholar and naturalist, young Hans Sloane. The clergy in Killyleagh at that time kept their eyes open for young people who showed potential and Hans certainly fell into this category. As it so happens Killyleagh, shortly after the time when Hans eventually departed for London, had a school of philosophy opened. It would have been a fitting addition to a village which was, at the time, an important and thriving location for the intelligentsia of the day.

Early Collections

Like all youngsters who lived in Killyleagh (and the same applies today) Hans loved to spend time along the shores of Strangford Lough. Within a few minutes from his house he would have been alongside the water exploring the shoreline for unusual objects which caught his eye. He was interested in plants and other marine objects. He was fascinated by the wonders of growth and eagerly searched the miles and miles of the shore. Often he went on his own and was totally wrapped up in his explorations. Before long he started to bring home bits and pieces of flotsam and jetsam which he had found floating in the water as well as all sorts of plants which grew alongside the lough. Perhaps without fully appreciating it at the time, Hans had commenced his life's work. Soon he had boxes containing stones and shells, glass jars filled with growing plants and even little bottles with live creatures inside. His brothers, as most older brothers do, considered that young Hans was just a bit odd and paid little attention to his ever burgeoning collections. But they soon realised that this was more than just a schoolboy fad. Their little brother had an eye for natural objects and seemed to delight in all living things.

He prevailed upon the boatmen around Killyleagh to take him out to the islands of the lough and there he revelled in the wonders of wild birds, their eggs and their nests. It was not before long that he travelled north along the rough roads, presumably on horseback, to Bangor where he found a local man to take him over to the Copeland Islands which lay just offshore at the mouth of Belfast Lough. There he discovered the ground nesting birds such as seagulls and terns where there was little or no space even to walk over the ground, such was the density of the nests. He collected eggs and other artefacts from the island and returned home thrilled at his adventure. He was only then in his early teenage years and it is remarkable to think that it would have taken him probably a couple of days just to get to the Copelands and back. Travel arrangements in the 1670s were rather more primitive than they are today. Thus was the determination shown by a boy who would, in his long lifetime, bring fame, if not exactly fortune, to Killyleagh.

In 1676 when he was 16 years old, Hans contracted an illness which almost certainly was tuberculosis. In those days cures for diseases were, if not unknown, then very rare. For the next three years Hans took great care of his health. He remained indoors and rarely ventured out. He ate temperately and avoided liquor. In terms of his life to come these early decisions about his eating and drinking habits were to stand him in good stead. Throughout his life he remained, if not absolutely abstemious, then certainly moderate in his drinking habits. One glass of wine was sufficient for Hans when all around him his friends would have overindulged and suffered the negative after-effects of a night's carousing.

These enforced years as a semi invalid were not wasted as one would imagine for such a sensible young man. He had his collections to peruse and examine and it was in these days that he refined the types of containers which were best to contain his ever more varied items. He even considered how best to classify and categorise them. He read all he could and kept contact with the rector at the parish church and with other interested people in Killyleagh.

Whilst his brothers were still around he got them to collect for him and, of course, when he was able to be out of doors again he wasted no time in getting down to the harbour and scouring the beaches for anything that interested him or caught his eye. He would have been a regular sight beachcombing with bags in his hands into which he would deposit his latest finds. He was a contented lad whose curiosity impressed his friends and neighbours. They often visited his house to discover what Hans has brought up from the shore. Their young friend had impressed them from an early age and they felt sure that he had a very bright future.

2.
Hans leaves Killyleagh for London – and then Jamaica

When Hans eventually recovered from his rather lengthy bout of illness, he made up his mind to depart for London. He had learnt much at home in county Down and his interest in botany and nature had been fired in his own home village. Advices given to him by the rector and by his friends indicated that a move to the big city was the wise action to take. He packed his bags and made the tortuous journey by land and sea to London.

He was by now 19 years old and was determined to study chemistry. He found accommodation at the Apothecaries Hall where he settled in. He was, from the start, a studious young man. He attended his lectures and undertook his study in a scholarly way but he still made time for his chief hobby, botany. Being in London meant that there were many great gardens to visit and Hans soon knew all the best places to pursue his interests. His collections grew but he made sure to get his priorities right.

He made two constant friends in John Ray (1627-1705), who was a naturalist, and Robert Boyle (1627-1691), who was a chemist and also an Irishman. Ray taught Hans the rudiments of cataloguing and Boyle engaged Hans in the discovery of cures and medicines. For the next four years Hans divided his time between studying and collecting and, by 1683, he had almost completed his medical course.

He decided to finish his doctor's degree in France. With two friends he sailed for France across the English Channel and took a coach to Paris. The French capital in those days of the late 17th century was a hotbed of intrigue. If the French were not actually at war with England, then they were on the verge of it. The populations of both countries could never rely on any lengthy period of peace although Hans fortunately arrived during one such period.

Hans spent the mornings each day studying the plants in the city gardens and parks and, in the afternoons, attended his lectures on botany, chemistry and anatomy, all of which of course were delivered in French. He was a model student and made steady progress towards his degree. 'Sloane was a physician by training and a collector by inclination'.[1] This truly summed up the young county Down man from Killyleagh. He was resolved to be a credit to those back home who had guided him in his early days after the death of his father and the absence of his mother.

As a Protestant, however, Hans now encountered a difficulty which he had probably not considered. Only Catholic students were permitted to complete their medical degrees at a French university. Protestants had either to go to a Dutch university or to the university at Orange. This was in a tiny principality, ruled over by a prince (at that time Prince William of Orange who would soon be the King of England). It was situated close to the town of Avignon and was always being threatened by the French kings who wanted to obliterate not only this insignificant little statelet, but also Protestants. It was a time of great persecution of Protestants by the French Catholics and so to go to Orange looked like a risky adventure. But Hans, still suffering slightly from the after-effects of his three year illness, decided to go south where the weather was warmer rather than freezing in the cold winter in the Netherlands.

It did not take long for Hans to graduate. In fact he only needed to be there for a matter of months before the degree was conferred upon him at Christmas 1683. He was now Dr Hans Sloane.

He was keen to further pursue his studies and opted to spend time at the university of Montpellier which was also in the south of France. Here he had more wonderful gardens to explore and his expertise continued to grow in this botanical Mecca. However his stay was to be suddenly curtailed owing to the continued persecution of the Protestants. He realised that, as he stood firm in his own faith, it was not safe for him to remain in France. He took the coach north to Paris where he bade farewell to the friends he had made there and hastened back to London.

He arrived safely by the end of May having, all things considered, succeeded in many of his endeavours. He had completed his degree and was now a doctor; he had experienced university life in three renowned universities and he had made friends amongst the French who were to remain close to him throughout his life. It had been a worthwhile experience and it gave yet more focus to a man who was to leave an indelible mark on the fabric of society in the British Isles and beyond. His steadfastness and thoughtfulness had endeared him to many people from whom he had learnt so much. His sojourn in France was to prove to be a cornerstone of his career in botany and medicine.

Setting up a medical practice and the chance of a lifetime – a journey to Jamaica

Hans had, naturally enough, returned to London weighed down with plants and artefacts collected during his stay in France. His dear friend, John Ray, was delighted that Hans had brought back so much and he was keen to examine his finds. Ray himself was, at that time, working on a great botanical work which would become the set course for all those who studied botany. Hans knew his collections from the continent would greatly assist Ray so he made sure to give many of his treasures to his friend. This is typical of the kind and generous man that Hans Sloane was to become. It would have been quite normal to keep one's own finds to oneself and then to make a name for oneself for their discovery. But Hans believed that anything he had that would help a friend should be shared for the greater good. He passed on as many of his discoveries as would be of assistance to Ray. John Ray was very grateful for Hans' help and was careful to acknowledge the help given to him by Sloane in his book.

Hans was becoming well known even though he had only just completed his degree and had not yet set up a medical practice. He was considered to be an asset to the Royal Society and, as such, was worthy of a place in their hallowed ranks. He was admitted to their number in 1685 when he was just 25 years old, one of their youngest ever members. At the same time the eccentric and renowned doctor, Thomas Sydenham, took a liking to the young man and offered him the position of his assistant. Hans gratefully accepted the post which he hoped would soon lead to the formation of his own practice. Two years later, in 1687, he was admitted as a fellow to the Royal College of Surgeons.

But before he could even set up his medical practice, he was offered a position which was as fortunate as it was remarkable. The Duke of Albemarle had been appointed as Governor of Jamaica. He also needed a personal physician and, having taken soundings from his medical friends, the Duke decided to offer the post to the young and, it has to be said, the inexperienced Dr Hans Sloane. He must have made quite an impression on the Duke for such a position to be offered to him. In all likelihood Hans was probably approached after the Duke had spoken to his acquaintances in the Royal Society. But should Hans take up the offer?

He sought the advice of the two people whom he thought should have an opinion. Dr Sydenham was against and John Ray in favour of the appointment. Sydenham thought Hans too raw and untried but Ray, immediately sensing the opportunity of Hans bringing back countless treasures from the West Indies, was all in favour. Hans, of course, realised the reasons behind Ray's obvious enthusiasm but also respected the great Doctor's reservations.

Hans himself then had to make his decision. He knew he would have plenty of chances to bring back exciting botanical discoveries from the Caribbean and he also realised that there were so many opportunities to come home with all sorts of remedies for diseases. In the end, this swayed him and he agreed to go.

But Hans was also a shrewd young man. Being so young and appreciating the opportunity being offered to him, Hans could easily have accepted any terms and conditions of service. So he approached the Duke and suggested an annual salary of

£600. He knew that this was a princely sum for the position and one which the Duke could easily have refused. However Albemarle seemed to know that Hans Sloane was the man for him and so he agreed to the demand. Hans' colleagues in the city were astounded that he had been offered such a handsome salary but they realised by now that Hans was a man who knew what he wanted and could prove that he was worthy of it.

Shortly afterwards Hans was given another appointment – that of 'Physician to the West Indian Fleet' – a government job which meant taking care of any medical emergencies aboard any of His Majesty's ships in the Caribbean. This would, in all likelihood, not be too onerous a task and Hans immediately accepted – the salary, £300 per annum. So he was ready to leave England with two fine salaries and all this before he had even found his own medical practice in London. Some thought him very lucky; the more astute considered him exactly the man for the job.

In those days when newly appointed Governors were setting sail for their overseas postings, they did not simply go aboard a ship destined for that location. They assembled a little fleet of ships. Accordingly the Duke was allocated *HMS Assistance* as his flagship together with two merchant ships which carried not only the supplies for the Governor's new station but also a number of soldiers and sailors to defend him in the event of attacks by pirate ships and to act as escorts on ceremonial occasions in Jamaica. And added to these vessels was the Duke's own private yacht which had his own personal staff and provisions aboard. The little flotilla was thus assembled and was ready to sail by the middle of September 1687.

The vagaries of the British weather then intervened and a great storm blew up in the English Channel. For days it prevented the ever anxious Governor from setting out for his Caribbean station. Not until the 19th was there an improvement in the weather when, at long last, the party raised sail and departed. This was to be a three month voyage and being on board a small wooden vessel in those days was a trial for those who had never been on such a journey before. As a doctor, Hans presumed that he would cope well with the sweeping waves and rocking motion of the ship. He did not. He was a bad sailor. From start to finish he suffered from seasickness which he found difficult to deal with. Yet he knew that, as the doctor aboard, he would be needed to assist the other passengers. Consequently he suffered in silence and eventually got the better of the constant malaise.

The fleet called at the island of Madeira where they went ashore for provisions. They found the islanders friendly enough although they were happy to get on their way. Island life seemed unduly primitive for aristocratic Englishmen as well as for their Irish Doctor Sloane.

Crossing the Equator was a time for fun and frivolity, especially for the sailors on a long voyage. But for passengers 'crossing the line' for the first time, these age-old nautical ceremonies often made them apprehensive and fearful. They were expected to dress up and participate in an initiation test. There were given two options to assuage the gods of the sea. They could either offer the seasoned crew members a decent amount of money for them to persuade the gods not to punish the innocents or they could accept the other alternative and be ducked three times into the sea. There was little argument for the first-timers, including Dr Sloane. They paid up and looked pleasant.

Before arriving in Jamaica, the party called at Barbados for some days. This was a pleasant interlude as the island was one of the loveliest in those climes. They enjoyed their stay and the Duke had his first opportunity of dressing up in all his regalia to pay his respects to the local Governor.

Opportunities not to be missed

Hans had now his first opportunity to pursue his hobby. He started collecting and it was a case of not knowing where to start, such was the abundance of botanical riches. He explored the ponds and the shorelines and, above all, he discovered the various and numerous indigenous animals and plants none of which he had ever seen before. He was in his element and considered his required presence upon the Governor at his soirees rather a waste of time – or at least time which he could have better used.

Throughout the entire voyage Hans had taken notes about everything he saw. The seabirds like the great albatrosses and the fish, many of which were caught and brought aboard. He was particularly impressed by the porpoises, dolphins, whales and sharks which he constantly watched as they sailed westwards. He was put out, of course, when the crewmen harpooned many of these fine creatures to supplement their food supplies. By the time he arrived at his destination, the good doctor's collections were already filling every corner of the ship. There were jars, boxes and bottles filled with little creatures, marine plants and other botanical items. By the time they left Barbados for their final destination, Hans' collections were already quite extensive.

Not long before the Governor's fleet arrived in Jamaica, they passed the tiny islands of St Kitts and Nevis. Hans was intrigued to discover that most of the inhabitants on these tropical islands were of Irish descent. Their ancestors had been brought there as convicts and they had now become model citizens in their Caribbean paradise. Certainly for Hans it was a most unusual discovery – to find his own country folk resident amidst the palms and sandy beaches of this faraway place. He thought it must not have been the worst location for criminals. They had certainly landed on their feet.

Arrival in Jamaica

When the Governor and his party had settled down in Government House in Port Royal as the capital was known in those days, Hans made sure to make proper medical arrangements for the Duke. Dr Sloane was ever attentive to the Governor.

Soon he set about exploring the area and found countless items to add to his collection. He enjoyed the company of the local people who were drawn to the good doctor and found him a most amenable and intriguing person. Hans learnt about their various customs and was often to be found at their ceremonies and tribal gatherings. He was keen to understand their ways and he carefully made copious notes on every subject concerning the lives of the island natives.

Some months after his arrival in Jamaica, in early 1688, Hans set out on a journey to the north of the island. He travelled on horseback with a good and reliable guide. In retrospect this might have been considered a rather dangerous undertaking but Hans probably did not even think about the possible pitfalls of taking such a journey into territory that was not only unknown to him but which could have been considered a highly risky adventure. But the magnet of all those plants and animals which he had not seen before was too much of an attraction for him. He rode for miles collecting as he went. He was soon burdened down with all his new acquisitions but was delighted with every additional artefact. He stayed in the huts of the natives who must have found him both kindly and, if truth were told, courageous.

One particular remedy which he found the natives using was a chocolate drink which they used as a cure for a 'lightness of the stomach'. Hans sampled the drink. It looked thick and rather unwholesome. In fact he did not much care for the taste so he decided to add milk and the outcome was an altogether more palatable drink. It was much sweeter and, above all, not so treacly. This was one of his principal discoveries which he brought back home. It was this particular recipe which the well-known drinks manufacturer, Messrs Cadbury, used for many years, right until the present day. Their hot chocolate drink became very popular in the middle of the nineteenth century when they used the same ingredients which Hans had found when he was in Jamaica in the 1680s.

Whilst he journeyed throughout the island on a trip that took many weeks, he encountered an earthquake. This must have been a frightening experience for him but, as with everything which was new to him, he revelled in the excitement of discovery. Exhausted, but supremely happy, Hans made his way back to the capital and to the Governor's residence.

However, upon his return, Hans was met with some terrible news. The young 34 year old Governor, the Duke of Albemarle, had died despite having taken all the medication which Hans had prescribed for him. The Duchess and her staff attached no blame whatsoever to Dr Sloane for they realised that the Duke's frailty could have, and sadly did, hasten his demise.

The Duchess wanted to return to England as soon as possible. She had no wish to stay in this hot and steamy climate. Consequently she sent letters back to the King and to the Foreign Office in London requesting permission to return. But correspondence took months to arrive back in England. Not only did it take most of three months for a ship to sail there but it also took time for an available ship to appear. It was not until March 1689 that the party eventually bade farewell to Jamaica.

As the Duchess had no intention of burying her late husband in Jamaica, so his body had to be embalmed and it fell to Hans to carry out Her Grace's instructions. The Duchess had a great affinity with Hans and she had no objections to him bringing back all his collections aboard her fleet of ships which sailed out of Port Royal harbour in the last days of March.

In the 15 months which Hans had spent in the Caribbean he had made numerous notes; he had corresponded with his friends, Ray and Boyle, in London and he had gathered numerous items to bring home. He had plants in boxes; butterflies pasted between the pages of great albums; he had specimens carefully set into bottles and jars of every shape and size. And he had three live animals which he hoped might survive the long journey back home.

Firstly he had a live snake in a large jar which was making good progress until it managed to escape on to the deck of the ship, only to be shot dead by a terrified member of the crew. Secondly he had a lizard, or perhaps it was an iguana, in a sturdy pen. Hans thought it was thriving and eating well – and so it was until it struggled free from its cage and jumped over the side of the ship to its death. He then had only one animal left – his crocodile which was also kept on a large cage. Although it seemed to be prospering on rats and other vermin captured aboard ship, it was found dead one morning. There appeared to be no reason for its sudden death. And so Hans had to return with no living specimens from his trip to the West Indies. However, he did have plenty of other collections which were to enthral the scientific world for many years.

Apart from his chocolate drink cure, there was another remedy which helped the medical world for many years. The bark of the Peruvian pine which was found in abundance in Jamaica (and, of course, in other parts of south America) produced quinine which was popularised by him and was widely used as a tonic and as an anti-malarial drug with much success then, as now.

The journey home was not without incident. They had to beware of privateers on the high seas as there was always the possibility of their ship being attacked and captured. They encountered a French ship which they were about to seize. However they were uncertain whether or not France was at war with England at that time and the captain decided that discretion was the better part of valour and therefore did not take the prize which could have contained great wealth.

Although the time spent in Jamaica was much shorter than Hans could have anticipated there is no doubt whatsoever that his sojourn there, amongst the tribesmen of the island and its splendid gardens, was the turning point of his career. When he came home he was barely 30 years old and yet had made a great name for himself throughout the world of science in the British Isles and further afield. He could now look forward to a glittering career set amongst the scions of botany and collections. Hans Sloane was already a household name. It was now up to him to capitalise on his new found fame.

Return to English shores

Owing to the political uncertainties of the time the crew on board the fleet returning Hans and the Duchess of Albemarle to home shores was not certain who was on the throne. Such was the situation that the crew of a small boat intercepted off the Cornish coast was questioned as to who was King. Much to the relief of those on board it was discovered that the Glorious Revolution had taken place with King William and Queen Mary on the throne.

Consequently they realised that it would be perfectly safe to come ashore and travel on to London. Once in the capital Hans was prevailed upon by the Duchess to remain in her service for the time being. Although this meant that he still could not set up his own medical practice Hans was quite amenable to stay with her. This would mean that, apart from some relatively minor medical duties to perform to ensure the health of the Duchess and the rest of her staff, Hans could now spend his time collecting. He was to spend four further years in the Duchess' household up to the year 1693. For part of this time he lived at Montagu House which, after his death in 1753, was to become the first permanent home of the British Museum.

During 1690, the year after his return, there was an event which was to prove to be most significant to Hans and many others. King William, the same man who, as Prince William, ruled over the principality of Orange where Hans gained his medical degree, set sail for Ireland where he comprehensively defeated the Catholic forces of King James at the Battle of the Boyne. The victory ensured the continued reign of a Protestant monarch on the throne of Great Britain and Ireland. His former friends and neighbours back in Killyleagh were as ecstatic as their famous son, Hans Sloane.

3.
Hans Sloane – the Physician

In 1693 Hans left the employment of the Duchess of Albemarle. He was anxious to set up his own medical practice and, probably with the help and influence of his old friend Thomas Sydenham, he acquired a very fine and elegant house at 3 Bloomsbury Place where he immediately started to attract many wealthy and eminent patients. In fact he was soon to have on his books many members of the Royal family. It seems hard to comprehend that, as a first time medical practitioner and without having the experience

Sloane's 21st century statue in Hans Sloane Square, Killyleagh

of attending patients in their own homes, Hans should have, so soon, welcomed royalty to his surgery. He was, without doubt, a young man who had landed firmly on his feet.

In his book 'Sir Hans Sloane, the Great Collector and his Circle', E. St. John Brooks epitomises the kind of man that Hans was. 'He was a fashionable physician – one judges him a cautious and competent doctor; in botany an accomplished amateur; obviously an enthusiastic and tireless worker both at his profession and his hobby'.[2]

Now that he had settled into his medical practice Hans decided to marry. He was now 35 years old and he felt the time was opportune to have a good wife by his side. When he was in Jamaica he had made the acquaintance of a wealthy young couple, Fulk and Elizabeth Rose. Fulk Rose had made a fortune in the West Indies and the future looked bright for himself and his family. However he died out in Jamaica leaving his wife to look after their four daughters. The widow Rose and her family returned to England on the same ship as Hans. The friendship turned to romance and, on 11 May 1695, Hans and Elizabeth were married in London. The new Mrs Sloane and her children moved into 3 Bloomsbury Place and this was to remain their home throughout their married life together until Elizabeth died, aged 66, in 1724.

Elizabeth had been left a very wealthy woman. She had been bequeathed a large portion of her late husband's considerable fortune and, added to that, she had inherited her late father's estate. As far as finances were concerned there were never any problems in this regard for Hans Sloane. He was a model stepfather who got on famously with his stepdaughters. When he and Elizabeth had, in course of time, children of their own there was ample love all round for his growing family. Elizabeth and Hans had four children themselves, three daughters, Sarah, Elizabeth and Mary and one son, Hans. Sadly little Hans and their youngest daughter, Mary, died in infancy leaving the good doctor and his wife with six daughters at home. The cause of death for his two children is not recorded but one can assume that they died of a childhood disease which today would never even have affected them. For such a fine doctor who had himself made so many advances in medical care, it must have been galling and humbling to lose two of his own children. But he accepted the inevitability that many youngsters would continue to die until inoculations and vaccinations would put an end to such unnecessary deaths in infants.

Hans' practice flourished as he continued to make a name for himself. He was able to charge upwards of a guinea an hour to his rich clientele. They were happy to pay for the services of such a distinguished and competent physician. As ever there was the other more caring and generous side to Doctor Sloane. From the very beginning of his practice days he provided free care to patients who were too poor to pay for their own treatment. He always felt that there was a real need for doctors to treat all types and conditions of men and women. He continued to provide this service throughout his lengthy career. The poor, as well as the privileged, received medical care which was second to none. They realised and appreciated the kind of man which Hans Sloane undoubtedly was.

Hans and his wife enjoyed the company of their friends who were often invited to dine at 3 Bloomsbury Place. Hans was a bon viveur but was never a heavy drinker. And this was at a time when those with money and influence tended to overeat and over imbibe. Hans revelled in fun and discussion with his friends without jeopardising his health and his abstemiousness laid a firm foundation for his long and interesting life.

However there was one problem for the family at 3 Bloomsbury Place. With two parents, six daughters, a fairly large staff and a huge numbers of collections crammed into their fine dwelling house there needed to be some room for expansion if they were going to continue to be the ideal and consummate couple and family. Hans decided to take over the house next door – number 4 Bloomsbury Place. The rent for both houses was £15 per annum which, hard as it is to believe, was an enormous outgoing in the early years of the 18th century. But the Sloanes could easily afford this expenditure and they knew it would be an ideal location for Hans' ever expanding collections. In this fashionable part of London the Sloanes had some very eminent neighbours, one of whom was the designer of St Paul's Cathedral, Sir Christopher Wren.

Hans cherished his profession and also the fact that he could take time to add to his wonderful collections. As always he was happy to share his new finds and the cures he was discovering with those around him. He never saw any sense in keeping these improvements to himself. He saw discoveries as being of use to all mankind and the more that people knew of them then the sooner diseases would be eradicated. If only his philosophy could have been shared by all doctors and collectors. Too many of them kept their findings secret thus depriving medical science of much earlier breakthroughs in the form of cures for debilitating illnesses and ailments.

Hans Sloane's friends were anxious that he should publish the findings from his trip to Jamaica and the West Indies and, at last, in the late 1690s the first volume of his 'Natural History of Jamaica' appeared. It was immediately ranked amongst the best and most instructive books in its field. It took Hans a further quarter of a century to publish the second volume in 1725.

The Jamaican Doctor

Hans was always affectionately known by this name – the Jamaican doctor. He continued to give his services free of charge to those who could not afford to pay but he soon realised that it was not worthwhile for his poor patients to receive care from him if they had to pay for their prescriptions. They could not afford to pay the apothecaries who dispensed the medicines. Hans set out to remedy this anomaly. In 1696 he organised for a dispensary to be opened close to his practice where the medicines could be dispensed at cost price. He was never able to get the poor a totally free service but he had done more than any other person to make life tolerable for those who could least afford to make payments. The greatest obstacle he encountered was the position of the apothecaries themselves. They were intransigent and refused to countenance a free service even to those in direst need. In the end these medicine sharks prevailed and free prescriptions remained a long way off for the poor and needy.

Hans' generosity knew no bounds. When he was appointed a Physician to Christ's Hospital in 1694, he was offered a salary of £30 per annum. He accepted the payment but immediately donated the entire amount back to the hospital for the benefit and care of its patients. He held the post for 36 years until 1730 and one can therefore appreciate the total care given to their patients over all these years. In fact one of those people who benefited was the diarist, Samuel Pepys, in the days before his fame had spread.

The Jamaican doctor was, of course, that same doctor from Killyleagh. His friends and relatives in county Down and throughout Ireland, realising what a talented relation they had, took to writing to him seeking remedies for their own ailments. Hans was happy to oblige and so he entered into lots of correspondence prescribing medicines and giving medical advice. It was much appreciated. There is little correspondence, however, that gives any clue as to whether or not he ever visited any of his family in Ireland. There is speculation that he may have come over for visits in the later years of his life but it may well be that he never returned.

Attendance on Queen Anne

Hans attended many peers of the realm and their families and was then appointed as Physician extraordinary to Queen Anne in 1712. She was the unfortunate monarch who lost over a dozen children in infancy and whose health was continually a matter of concern to her courtiers as well as to her people. Hans Sloane attended the Queen on numerous occasions and was present at her deathbed in 1714. This was a critical time for the British monarchy. Since none of her children ever attained their majority, the question of her successor was critical to the nation. It seemed possible that the hated Jacobites might return to the throne unless the Queen herself signified otherwise. Those in favour of a return to a Catholic monarch hovered as the Queen breathed her last. She had not even the power to sign her name to ensure the Protestant Hanoverian succession. Their cause seemed lost. But they had not reckoned with the good doctor from Killyleagh.

Hans Sloane is considered to be the saviour of the Protestant succession for it was he who was able to keep the Queen alive long enough for her to make her vital signature. The Queen died not long afterwards but, by dint of his medical skill, Doctor Hans Sloane, kept her alive long enough to keep out the Jacobites for ever. Everyone realised what a close call it had been.

A baronetcy for Hans Sloane

The first Hanoverian monarch, King George I, ascended the throne shortly after the death of the ill-fated Queen Anne. Many of his new subjects had ensured his smooth transition from Germany to London. In 1716 he announced that Doctor Hans Sloane had been made a baronet and so it was that Sir Hans Sloane became one of the first doctors ever to be so honoured. Hans and his family were rightly and justifiably proud of the accolade. The nation itself was delighted that their new monarch should have elevated one of its most favoured citizens in such a tangible way.

During this second decade of the 18th century further honours were bestowed upon Sir Hans. He received doctorates from such worthy universities as Edinburgh and Oxford but the one which pleased him most of all was the degree awarded to him by Trinity College in Dublin. Records at that time were incomplete and it is not exactly clear when Hans did receive this award. However there is little doubt that the degree was bestowed – it is simply that the relevant records have not survived.

In 1716 Hans was also appointed Physician General to the Army probably, once more, on the recommendation of the King himself. This was a purely honorary post but it was just one more step on Hans' rise to fame and fortune.

The Presidency of the Royal College of Surgeons

Hans remained totally focused in his pursuit of excellence and improvement in medicine and in the expansion of his famous collections. In 1719, when he was 59 years old, he was elected the President of the College of Surgeons. This was a most prestigious appointment and one sought by every physician of note in the country. For 16 years he held the post and he proved, as could only be expected, to be a most efficient holder of the title.

Under Hans' leadership the college pursued much needed reforms in the rationalisation of prescriptions but, more importantly, he persuaded the college finally to discard superstitious medicines and even more dangerous quack remedies. It seems hard to believe that such eminent men as Sloane and his contemporaries were still struggling with quacks and medical impostors well into the 18th century. Yet there were many so-called doctors who continued this scandalous practice simply to feather their own nests. Money and profit accrued from decidedly unsafe potions still seemed to be the driving force for many in the medical profession at that time. Hans Sloane was able to lead his colleagues in their successful drive to eradicate these selfish and greedy operators and to set a firm foundation for the worthy and proven medicines which took British physicians into the forefront of all medical research throughout the world.

Hans Sloane's simple and uncomplicated approach to prescribing for ailments continued to be met with ridicule amongst those with a vested interest in selling worthless ingredients for medicines but he was successful in ignoring their attentions and, with the College behind him, he soon cleared out those criminal elements from the medical profession. His pioneering approaches in this regard will always be remembered by a grateful College of Physicians.

The discovery of inoculation

In this day and age we all understand and appreciate the benefits of inoculation against many diseases. When we ever think about it we understand that we are actually being injected with a small amount of a disease itself so that our immune system can build up the necessary defences against it.

In the early years of the 18th century it was Doctor Sir Hans Sloane who was one of the pioneers in the use of inoculation. He advocated its use in many circumstances and, by way of proving how crucial it was, ensured that his own children were amongst the first to be inoculated against a number of childhood diseases. He was always prepared to show his confidence in new cures and discoveries in the fight against illness and crippling disease by encouraging his own family to take the consequent remedies.

And he was not alone in his endeavours. The King himself, who seemed to know Hans well, insisted that the royal princes and princesses were also inoculated. This action was the catalyst which ensured the widespread use of this practice. Had it not been for the advocacy of the monarch and Hans Sloane, it could have taken many more years to prove the undoubted benefits of inoculation to a sceptical population. Thus it was that this method of combating childhood diseases remained in force until Jenner eventually discovered vaccination.

Back in the north of Ireland, in Newcastle in county Down not far from Killyleagh, a certain Doctor Magnus Prince was also advocating the use of inoculation and there were relatives of Hans Sloane who were treated by Dr Prince. Hans was in regular correspondence with him and also with members of his own family over the pros and cons of the use of inoculation.

In 1729 it was probably the case that Hans did travel over to Belfast (then a very small and insignificant place – Killyleagh itself would have been of more importance) to meet Prince and to discuss the latest medical discoveries, as well as, of course, talking about the importance of inoculation. This would have been a difficult trip to venture across the Irish Sea for a man who was 69 years old. But Hans must have considered the journey worth making. Magnus Prince was a medical pioneer just as Hans Sloane was and was doubtless experiencing opposition which Hans was able to deflect by being present in county Down himself. These assumptions may not be totally accurate but they certainly are worthy of belief.

Hans' energy for excellence in his profession was unbounding. A problem for many young children was weak and bent bones. Many youngsters ended up with crooked or bow legs which impeded their ability to walk properly. We know nowadays about the condition called rickets caused by vitamin D deficiency and we know how it was eliminated many years ago. But in Hans' day the best remedy he could suggest was to recommend to parents that they did not encourage their children to walk too soon. It was thought that if the body weight of a child was exerted on its legs too soon then they would simply buckle under the pressure. This will seem almost incredible for us to comprehend today but such were some of the struggles which physicians of Hans' era had to deal with.

Hans Sloane will be remembered then, as now, as being a man of foresight, of courage and of determination. He was generous to a fault; he remained the friend and physician to the rich and poor, to King as well as pauper; he kept his head when all around him were losing theirs. This medical genius from Killyleagh had laid the foundations of a health service in the latter years of the 17th century which remain as fresh and keen today as they were at the height of his career in the 1700s.

4.
Hans Sloane – the Collector

Hans Sloane was an incredibly talented and caring doctor; but Hans Sloane was also the world's greatest collector. His zeal for cataloguing and listing items of scientific and botanical interest was without equal. In 1685, aged just 25, and 2 years before he left for Jamaica, he was elected to the Royal Society. It is interesting to note the reason for the formation of such an association. Its tenets held as fast in 1685 as they do today.

> *'The Royal Society is the independent scientific academy of the United Kingdom dedicated to promoting excellence in science. It plays an influential role in national and international science policy and supports developments in science, engineering and technology in a wide range of ways.'*

Hans was an ambitious member of the society. Within a year or two he was vying for a position on its committee. In 1693 he was finally elected as one of its two secretaries, one of the most important and onerous of all committee posts. He had not only to attend as many of the meetings as he could to take the minutes, but he also had to prepare lots of working papers for the committee members to discuss. Then, as nowadays, the secretary was the one upon whom most of the work fell, but was also the least glamorous of all the committee positions. As an example of his workload it is noted that in 1703 there were 43 meetings of the Society's committee. Hans attended on 37 occasions whilst the President turned up only three times — a great attendance record for the tireless secretary; an abysmal one for the seemingly disinterested chairman.

At the time of Hans' acceptance of the post of secretary, the Royal Society was in the doldrums. It had lost its momentum and even its reason for existence was under question. Hans Sloane soon put an end to this lethargy and uncertainty and set about revitalising the Society. He was determined to put this celebrated association back into the mainstream of the world of scientific academia. He succeeded in his endeavours despite the fact that his own medical practice suffered. But he was the right man for the job; he was patient and assiduous as well as being able and friendly in his dealings with people. The Society was in a safe pair of hands.

By 1703 the famous Sir Isaac Newton was the Society's President and other notable members included Edmond Halley, discoverer of the famous comet, and Samuel Pepys. Under Newton's and Sloane's leadership the Society was soon back to its former prominence and began to move from strength to strength. Hans was liked by the members and admired by many scholars.

However, in such circumstances where the secretary was a luminary and a skilled communicator there was always the opportunity for clarion voices to be heard railing against the efforts of such a fine administrator. Within the Society's members was a particularly jealous and antipathetic man called Dr John Woodward. He was an irascible man who seemed to spend his time complaining and causing difficulties to members of the committee – particularly to the secretary, Dr Hans Sloane. He continued to be a troublesome member who actually fought a duel with another member during the early years of the 18th century. At length the Society decided that the only option left to them was to expel Woodward from the Society's membership – and he was summarily dismissed with no recourse to rejoin. At last the committee could, once more, spend its time considering what was best for the Royal Society rather than having to think of the recalcitrant Dr Woodward at the commencement of business at each and every one of their meetings. A sigh of relief was almost audible at the first gathering following Woodward's expulsion.

Hans' clarity of vision never to see the truth or the Society's principles compromised earned him eternal respect in the eyes of the members of the Society. In 1713, after twenty years as secretary, he decided to resign. When Newton resigned as President in 1727, there was only one clear successor – Sir Hans

Sloane. He was duly elected and remained in this post until 1741, when he passed on the President's baton at the age of 81. He had been a most invaluable committee member for almost half a century, a period neither surpassed nor equalled.

The improvement to the Society's collections

Hans Sloane's energies were inexhaustible. He was totally focussed in his endeavour to make the Royal Society the most prestigious organisation in the country. But such a society had to have a collection second to none. Sadly, for many years, the collections in the Society's repository had been neglected. It was not that new additions were not regularly being offered to the Society. But the collection had become untidy, muddled and poorly catalogued.

Hans took the matter in hand and insisted that properly qualified personnel were employed whose job it would be to systematically set out the valuable items in the collection and to display and list them in a clear and professional manner. As ever there were detractors who did not want to spend the money to sort out these national treasures but Hans persisted and soon the repository was brought up to scratch. By doing so, the Society once more became the place where explorers and collectors from all over the world insisted on placing their finds. The Royal Society had regained its respected position where the biggest and best in the natural discoveries of the world were once more to be found.

Hans Sloane's reputation had spread throughout the world and every university and seat of learning was clambering to honour the redoubtable Sir Hans Sloane. And so, from the early 1700s until his death in 1753, he was invited to accept decorations and degrees from such cities and states as Paris, Prussia, St Petersburg and Madrid. Even in 1752 the university of Gottingen elected Hans a fellow, just months before his death. There was hardly a city in western Europe which had not honoured him in some way or another.

In 1741 when he indicated that he wanted to stand down as President of the Society, it was quite a struggle for him to do so. The members tried to persuade him to stay on but, as his health was deteriorating, they felt obliged to agree, albeit reluctantly, to his standing down. However he remained a member of the Society right up to his passing. He was to be a member for almost 68 years – the longest time for any man then or even today.

The name of Sir Hans Sloane remains amongst the most prominent and best remembered of all the members of the Society throughout its centuries of service to the country. It is greatly indebted to him for holding the Society together and keeping it in the public eye over so many critical years in the 17th and 18th centuries.

Contributions to the world of science

Hans Sloane will be remembered for the many varied aspects of his brilliant career. As a man of science in general, and of botany in particular, he was outstanding. His botanic fame, of course, took root during those early days when he was in the West Indies. In many ways he could count himself very fortunate at having had the opportunity to start his valuable collections whilst he was there. Being there during his twenties gave him a head start over all his contemporaries.

Most of his friends were only too glad that such a generous man as Hans was the one collecting in such a botanical paradise as Jamaica and its neighbouring exotic islands. Others, however, were never quite so pleased; some were intensely jealous that it was Hans Sloane and not they who had opened up the treasures of the Caribbean. In retrospect, especially for the general scientific world, it was probably just as well that such an opportunity fell to Hans as he was, from the outset, the kind of collector who wished everyone to benefit from his discoveries. One shudders to think of the potential difficulties had some of the more secretive and introvert explorers discovered these exciting early finds.

We know that it was Hans Sloane who first introduced the careful and deceptively simple method of plant cataloguing. In this day and age decent cataloguing and listing are taken for granted. But, in his day, collections were usually just thrown together. People were too anxious that items could be viewed without the foresight of proper classification.

His two volumes concerning his discoveries in the West Indies took too long to produce but, at least by 1725, the work did see the light of day and became a seminal work for botanists and scientific collectors.

For such an expert in the natural sciences, it is amusing to note that there was almost a comic side to his activities. In the 1730s, when he was already into his 70s, Hans looked after a Gambian slave who had been captured in his youth, taken to America and then brought to London. The reasons for Hans having this very unusual visitor are obscure although we can surmise that the experience helped both Hans and his guest. Not long after this visit, Hans had at his home, again as guests, an Indian tribal chief and his entourage, including the chief's wife. There would have been some inquisitive interest in this fashionable part of London to know that the good doctor Sloane had yet more exotic visitors. Yet again, naturally enough, both parties would have benefited from the experience.

Doctor Sloane also kept pets at home, including a porcupine and a beaver. Perhaps he kept cats and dogs as well.

The great collections

Sir Hans Sloane's collections were, by far, the most comprehensive – then as now. Each individual collection was rarely the largest of its kind and there were parts which did not hold any great interest to Sloane. In fact his excellent antiquities collections from Egypt, Greece and Rome – which would have enthralled others – were of no particular interest to him.

The first British Museum, as such, was the Ashmolean in Oxford, founded in 1683 just at the time when Sloane was graduating and entering the world of science. William Charlton, whose name was prominent at that time, owned a most wonderful private collection with an astounding array of material. His, however, was one of those higgledy-piggledy collections which had been rather erratically set up just to get people in to see what he had on show. Nonetheless it was such a great collection that Hans Sloane bought it in later life. Hans always had a good eye as well as professional acumen in abundance to seek out the finest purchases. Throughout his entire lifetime he added to his own collections many smaller ones which greatly enhanced those he already owned. Other collections were bequeathed to him and, by continually buying items as well, he ensured that every opportunity was taken to improve the exhibits which were already in his possession.

As he increased his acquisitions Hans made sure that the population could come to his museums not only to view the exhibits but, more importantly, to come to study and to be educated. The public was appreciative of the opportunities offered to them by Hans Sloane for there were very few institutions at that time willing to let the ordinary people in to study their precious collections. Once more we can see the foresight, generosity and magnanimity of the man from Killyleagh. It was in his own native village, after all, that he had been encouraged to search and collect and where he had discovered minor cures for himself; it was on the shores of Strangford Lough that he had seen the locals chewing seaweed as a cure for scurvy and it was in his own house in Frederick Street that he had first used bottles and jars to preserve the various plants and creatures he had found so close to home. His chief aim in life was always to share his discoveries.

Following his journey to Jamaica, Hans' zeal for collecting artefacts from those far-off places rubbed off on many others including the men at the Admiralty. It was not long before ships' captains were required to bring back as many new specimens from their destinations as possible. Sailors were encouraged to bring aboard whatever plant or unusual animal that they had found whilst ashore. It was not long before exploration parties of simple sailors were eagerly trudging through island jungles to make more and more striking and bizarre discoveries. Sometimes these precious cargoes were lost on the journey home when their ships were taken as prizes by an enemy. Of course, they could often add to their botanical booty when they themselves captured some unsuspecting merchantman on the high seas on their return to British waters. There is no doubt that these collecting activities certainly added to the excitement of life aboard ship in the 18th century.

Hans always took pride in preserving his plants as well as he could. Some of the seeds he collected during the 1680s were found to be growing until as late as the Second World War in the 1940s – a period of over 250 years. One wonders if seeds produced today will still be growing in the year 2250. His shells, fossils, insects and minerals have also kept relatively well after three hundred years. Items on view in the British Museum today, in the early years of the 21st century, were collected and catalogued by Hans Sloane himself all those years ago. We have much to thank him for and much to appreciate on account of his wonderful foresight.

Hans Sloane gathered together many great collections of paintings and books. He owned works by Albrecht Durer, Sir Henry Moore and by many other famous artists of the day. In the libraries of the Museum are shelves upon shelves of the finest books ever to have been written and still in their original leather-bound covers. It is almost possible to forget or underrate these marvellous collections because Sloane himself was never so keen on them. There are differing estimates as to the number of books which he collected. Some said 40,000 but, in the volume entitled 'Antient and Present State of County Down' published in Dublin in 1744 and dedicated to their own Sir Hans Sloane, its authors estimated that his book collection contained 69,352 books.

One particular and amazing item in his collection was a piece of the Giant's Causeway from county Antrim on the north coast of Northern Ireland. He even arranged for two additional 'joints' to be taken and presented to his friend, Sir Alexander Pope. One need hardly imagine the reaction of worthies in the field today if such a gift was made by a renowned collector to some latter day luminary. It seems that the gift to Pope was to enable him to further beautify his garden.

Hans welcomed not only the working public to his museum but also many well known personalities. Benjamin Franklin, on a visit to London, was most anxious to meet Sir Hans Sloane and the doctor duly obliged. On another occasion the composer, GF Handel, paid Hans a visit. However Handel literally blotted his copybook by placing a moist buttered scone upon a precious manuscript being shown to him by Hans. Doctor Sloane was said to have been livid.

Hans could not, of course, look after the collection on his own. He had various curators and assistants to do this job for him. Throughout the years these dedicated men classified and catalogued the specimens and assembled them in the best way possible for the visitors to view them. These were paid staff and the money to pay them came mainly from outside sources and from benefactors, but also from his own resources. Needless to say the displays could never have been properly set out without the talented assistance of these dedicated men.

From time to time there were burglaries at the museum. Items were stolen and on one occasion in 1700 thieves tried, mercifully unsuccessfully, to burn the museum down. The damage caused was slight but if the museum had been destroyed the future for such a collection would have been in jeopardy. As the years passed by improved security was introduced to ensure the safety of the world's greatest collections.

Hans' chief delight was to see people enjoying the specimens on display. He was praised for his work by many overseas visitors. They often got carried away by lauding the Sloane collections above those in their native countries. They knew Hans Sloane only too well. To encourage people to enter the museum's doors was his chief endeavour. The Sloane collections remained the place to visit and to expand one's own knowledge in the field of the sciences.

5.
The Good Doctor's Twilight Years

By the year 1742 Hans Sloane was already well into his 80s. Although in indifferent health he was, nonetheless, still very active both in the pursuit of his ever expanding collections and in his service to his fellow men. He had only recently resigned as President of the Royal Society. His wife had died 18 years previously but he remained in close contact with his two daughters and their families.

Some years earlier, in 1712, Hans had bought a house in the country. This was bigger than the usual 'house in the country'. It was the Manor House in Chelsea which, in those days, was a rather far out suburb of London. It was indeed a beautifully proportioned mansion which had connections with King Henry VIII and where the future Queen Elizabeth I had spent time as a child.

The house had remained as a weekend home for the Sloanes and they had travelled there regularly to take respite from the hustle and bustle of the city. The Apothecaries' Garden was in Chelsea and it was this secluded place which Hans loved most of all. There he spent many hours examining and enjoying the flowers and plants which abounded there. When he took over the Manor House he also became the landlord of the garden. He was pleased to permit the Royal Society of Apothecaries to make as much use of the garden as they wished on condition that they provided 50 new specimens of plants every year for 40 years. They were happy to do this and, after the 40 years, there were indeed 2,000 new botanical treasures scattered throughout the beautiful garden. Once more Hans Sloane had shown his great generosity as well as ensuring even more pleasure for those who visited the garden – as much for the poor as for the rich and privileged.

In future years, after his death, the apothecaries commissioned a fine statue of their benefactor which stands to this day in a prominent place within the garden.

In another gesture of magnanimity Hans donated additional ground which he owned at Chelsea to extend the graveyard at Chelsea Old Parish Church. This gift to the church was appreciated by the select vestry and by the townspeople. Hans' wife was buried in this graveyard in 1724. In due course of time he, too, would join his wife in those hallowed grounds.

The collections move to Chelsea

Before he moved to Chelsea, the Sloane collections at numbers 3 and 4 Bloomsbury Place were extensive. There was little room left where new additions could be located. What would Hans now do with regard to the museum? Would he let it remain in London under the care of his dedicated curators or would he move it down to the Manor House? He decided on the latter option and plans were set in train to dismantle the collections at Bloomsbury and pack them up for a move to Chelsea. This turned out to be a disaster and became the most complicated and hair-raising adventure of the century.

The responsibility for the move fell on the shoulders of one of his best curators, Edmund Howard. Hans himself went round his exhibition rooms and collected together the most precious and valuable pieces of jewellery as well as the smaller and important expensive objects. He carried these pieces with him on journeys to Chelsea in his carriage. Poor Howard had to push and cajole all sorts of delivery men with different sizes of carts and wagons. And for weeks on end the move continued slowly with Howard's temper becoming shorter and shorter. One can barely imagine the efforts made by Howard and the other curators. However, with encouragement and perhaps veiled threats from Doctor Sloane, the move was completed. The displays at the Manor House were superb and their surroundings much more conducive to showing off the nation's finest exhibits.

Hans continued to invite visitors to come to Chelsea to admire his collections. They came from every part of the globe and, for scientists arriving in England for any reason, one of their first ports of call for them was a visit to the great collections of Sir Hans Sloane. These men of letters regularly wrote fulsome reports in their native journals following their call with Hans and the examination of his many collections.

In his 89th year, 1749, a royal visit was made to view the collections. The Prince and Princess of Wales arrived and were suitably impressed by 'the good old gentleman' and his wide ranging displays. In his discussion with Hans, the Prince of Wales declared that the country itself should benefit from the collections. This greatly pleased Hans. The royal couple had been enthralled by what they had seen and wrote to Hans to thank him for his kindness.

Hans continued to spend as much time as he could in his garden. He was a little deaf although his mind continued to be acute and incisive. By now he owned a three-wheeled chair in which he was able to propel himself through the flowerbeds and across the lawns. It kept him quite independent although his staff were very fond of their kindly employer. The only slightly dissentient voice was that of the aforementioned Edmund Howard who found Sir Hans rather mean as far as money was concerned. No other member of staff ever complained about money. Maybe it was Howard trying to get back at his employer over the lengthy and difficult move of his collections from London to Chelsea.

Over the last years of his life more and more acquaintances and relatives from Ireland were seeking his assistance in placing their sons in positions either in the Navy or in offices in London. They knew that he would help if he could and they were rarely disappointed. Hans Sloane did have influence in so many businesses and there were many young people who owed a great deal by the intervention of this great doctor. The author E. St John Brooks sums up the situation very well. 'And so in their thousands the letters came pouring in, from all sorts and conditions of men, a veritable cross section of the varied society with which Sloane came in contact during more than half a century: from patient and country doctor, peasant and peer, duchess and servant, crank and lunatic, from beggar and even from felon'.[3]

This epitomises what an extraordinary man Sloane was. Even into his 90s he still had time to consider what help he could give and the energy to offer the assistance requested. Most people would long since have cast such begging letters into the waste bin.

What was to become of his collections?

His last years were spent considering where his collections should be placed after his death. There were many vested interests and many voices clamouring for his attention. He realised that his collections were the most wide-ranging anywhere in the world and how important it was to come to the correct decision.

First of all he thought that his family could inherit the exhibits but he immediately dismissed this idea because of the strain it would put on his daughters and their husbands. This could never offer a permanent solution and so he dropped this idea.

Secondly he pondered that the Royal Society could be the recipients but, because of their problems over finances, Hans reckoned that this would not be the wisest solution either.

Thirdly there was the possibility that the great Ashmolean Museum might be the answer, but again he did not consider that this was the right solution.

In the end he devised a cunning and sensible plan. This decision was probably the greatest contribution he ever made – as far as his excellent collections were concerned. In his will of 1739, when he was 79 years old, Hans insisted that his collections be kept intact and were to remain in London or close by. This immediately prevented the collections from being needlessly split up. In later codicils to his will he firmed up his arrangements and placed the museum in the care of trustees and the King, on behalf of the nation. In offering the collections he placed a price on them at £20,000. This money was to be divided between his two daughters. Although this was a considerable sum in those days, Hans Sloane had ensured that the true worth of his collections should be reflected not just in theory but also in terms of monetary value. Some may have thought that he was being mercenary but, quite the opposite, he was placing a value on his works which would make people think before paying the account.

He was wise enough to consider alternatives should the Crown refuse to make the purchase. If the King did turn down the offer, then the collections were to be offered in turn (and at the same price) to the Royal Society, Oxford University, the College of Physicians in Edinburgh, the Royal Academy in Paris, and finally to the universities in St Petersburg, Berlin and Madrid. Failing acceptance by any of these seats of learning, then the collections were to be publicly auctioned. He had made his choices.

On 11 January 1753, in the reign of King George II, Sir Hans Sloane died at Chelsea and was buried in the Chelsea Old graveyard in his family vault on the 19th. The oration at his funeral service was delivered by his friend, Dr Zachary Pearse, the Bishop of Bangor. The great Hans Sloane had passed on after a life filled with kindness and care.

Hans Sloane has left a legacy second to none. As a physician he banished superstition and introduced proper medical cures; as a scientist, he was eminent and, as a collector, his was the household name. His 92 years had been spent in the service of men, of high and of lowly station. His name would be remembered throughout the generations. And so it has been. The people of Killyleagh in county Down had lost their most famous son. They were rightly proud of their association with such a paragon of scientific excellence.

The establishment of the British Museum

Hans Sloane had appointed almost 70 trustees to prepare for the disposal of his collections – for wherever they were destined. The executors of his will called these trustees together within a few days of his death. The future of his irreplaceable specimens was uppermost in their minds. While the matters were being discussed, only the most valuable jewels had been temporarily removed from the collection and deposited in a bank vault for security. The executors and trustees fervently hoped that a speedy decision would be made to bring the collections into the public domain.

However the first reaction from the King was that there was unlikely to be enough spare money in the Exchequer to purchase Sloane's collections. The small sum of £20,000 was proving to be an obstacle. The executors needed to work quickly. The MPs amongst the trustees were given the task of bringing a Bill for the necessary funds before Parliament. The burden fell on Edward Southwell, MP for Bristol, to make the preparations. In his case he proposed that, at least until a permanent home was found for the collections, then they were to remain at the Manor House to enable the public to continue to view the exhibits. This seemed important lest, during any unforeseen delays, the collections were closed, even for a short period. Out of sight would have meant out of mind.

After several lengthy debates at Westminster the trustees were able to breathe a sigh of relief when, on 19 March 1753, the Bill to effect the purchase of Sir Hans Sloane's collections was passed. It was agreed that the collections were to be kept 'entire' and that they would continue to be open to the public.

Furthermore the new institution into which the Sloane collections were to be placed was to be known as the British Museum. The money for the purchase was to be raised by a public lottery, a decision which dismayed more than a few members of the trustees. Many considered that the new museum had been founded grudgingly and set up parsimoniously. Many also doubted that the funds would ever be raised in this manner.

The lottery was the usual story of corruption and chicanery but, in the end, £95,000 was accrued to run the Museum.

The British Museum was thus founded with the Sloane collections, comprising the major part, together with the collections of valuable manuscripts and books of Sir Robert Cotton and Robert Harley, Earl of Oxford. The museum's first home was at Montagu House in Bloomsbury close to the Sloanes' former home at Bloomsbury Place in the city. The doors first opened 6 years after Hans' death on 15 January 1759. Those wishing to visit were required to obtain a ticket but this requirement permanently ended in 1805.

Thus was founded the British Museum. The whole country was now able to take full advantage of his wonderful collections but its lasting memorial was that 'the treasure which Sloane bequeathed to his country and which is now purchased for it by parliament may be attended with numberless advantages to the public'.[4]

The Sloane memorial at Killyleagh Castle

Sir Henry Blackwood

1.
A Surprise Career in the Royal Navy

Shortly after Christmas 1770, in the tenth year of the reign of King George III, a little boy was born in Killyleagh castle, the stately home at the top of the main street in the small county Down fishing village. He was named Henry and was the eleventh child, and seventh son, of the owner of the castle, Lady Dorcas Blackwood and her husband, Sir John. The Blackwoods first child, Robert, had been born in 1755 and, unusually for families in the 18th century, all the children attained their majorities – there were no childhood deaths.

Killyleagh Castle was the second home of the Blackwoods, their other seat being Ballyleidy House not far from Bangor, a thriving market town on the county Down shore of Belfast Lough. Lady Dorcas, who was a baroness in her own right – something very rare in the British hereditary system – decided that, as she had more servants in the castle and much more space, it seemed the wise course of action to be delivered of her last child there.

And so it was. Sir John and his wife had set out by coach and four from Ballyleidy in good time for the confinement although it did take over two days to make the journey. Roads from the north of county Down to the Strangford Lough shore at Killyleagh, although tolerably good, were little better than rough dirt roads. Overnighting on the way, the Blackwoods were relieved to arrive in Killyleagh just in time for the Christmas festivities. Snow threatened but as the entourage swung through the gates of the castle, the staff were on hand to take care of their mistress. Many of Lady Dorcas' confinements had taken place at the castle in previous years so the preparations were well rehearsed. The child was born on the 28th of December 1770. Lady Dorcas was 44 years old and her husband in his 49th year.

The Blackwoods and Killyleagh

Killyleagh was a very important place from the early 17th century onwards and the position of the Blackwood family in relation to Killyleagh was of the utmost significance. On 10 March 1612, almost 400 years ago, King James I issued a Charter to Killyleagh which entitled it, amongst other privileges, to send two MPs to parliament, firstly in London and subsequently, from 1782 until 1800, to the Irish Parliament sitting in Dublin. Considering that Killyleagh had a population of less than 2,000 people, this was an impressive honour to say the least. Ireland, at that time, only sent a total of just over 100 MPs to Parliament and Killyleagh had two of these.

It was also entitled to have a provost (who was, almost without exception, either a member of the Blackwood family or one of their land agents) and 12 free burgesses. The men chosen to be Killyleagh's MPs came from the landed families of the county – Hamiltons, Sloans, Stevensons and, of course, Blackwoods. From 1761, nine years before Henry Blackwood was born, one of the MPs was Sir John Blackwood, Henry's father. He had been given an Irish baronetcy in 1763. He remained in post for 38 years until his death in 1799. Between 1776 and the year of the Irish Parliament's prorogation in 1800, no fewer than three of Henry's brothers, Robert, James and Hans, were also MPs alongside their father. For many years, therefore, two Blackwoods were firmly established as the local MPs.

The Blackwoods, like so many of the landed classes in the north east of Ireland, were of Scottish stock having settled in north county Down in the 17th century. At the outset, however, they were not considered members of the gentry and, in fact, were simply tenants of the Hamiltons. It was not long, however, until the family became landowners and, by the beginning of the 1700s, they owned no less than 6,000 acres.

Their original house at Ballyleidy did not match up to their new found status for it was only a simple two storey house, albeit set in wonderful surroundings. By the mid 18th century this anomaly had been resolved when a much grander, turreted mansion was erected on the site of their former home. It remained thus until it was destroyed by fire in 1796 whereupon the present house was built. The name of the house was changed to Clandeboye House in the time of the 6th baronet, (and first Marquess of Dufferin and Ava) Lord Frederick Temple Blackwood, in the mid 19th century. The family prospered and became much respected landowners throughout county Down. Henry's father's marriage to the wealthy Dorcas Stevenson had copper-fastened their position in Irish society.

The importance of Killyleagh in those years should not be underestimated. It was one of the seats of the county's foremost family. Regular reports were compiled by the Irish Corporation

Commissioners as to its circumstances. They listed the fact that Killyleagh continued to appoint its burgesses and that schools, a market house and even a temporary prison cell, known as the 'Black Hole', were functioning. A new pier was built although its erection courted controversy particularly amongst the townspeople. Lord Dufferin charged fees for boats unloading at the pier but the citizens disputed his right to levy a charge as the pier had been constructed between the high and the low water mark, making the soil on which it was built Crown land which ought not to have attracted fees from the landlord.

By the 1830s Killyleagh had its own mill which gave much needed employment to many of the townspeople. Regular markets were held and the town was booming by 1850. The factory chimneys and the turrets of the castle were then, as they are today, the most prominent symbols of the town. When people, on approaching Killyleagh from the Comber direction, see these landmarks, their hearts rise – they are home.

A favoured son

As the years progressed Henry spent as much time as he could in Killyleagh. Most of his education with his own private tutors had taken place at Ballyleidy but he was always glad when his father or one of his brothers brought him to the castle. He learnt to ride a horse early on and often used this mode of transport to come to Killyleagh. He enjoyed his holidays especially as he was able to get to know the sea and had many friends who took him out on the lough to fish and to learn about marine life. Killyleagh, in those days, was thriving and prosperous and down at the quay Henry spent many happy hours.

Having so many brothers was a mixed blessing for the young Henry. On the plus side he had plenty of tuition in riding to hounds, in hunting, in horse riding and in the varied pursuits of the gentry classes. His brothers, as they attained their majorities, had either taken Holy Orders (like his brother, John) or had entered the army. On the minus side, however, being a seventh son, although having its advantages, did also have its disadvantages, at least as far as a career was concerned. What would become of little Henry? The career options for him were somewhat limited.

The career decision for Henry was made by his father and his older brothers, for he would not have had much say himself. The consensus was to send Henry to sea. The family realised that Henry had enjoyed his time at the harbour and on the lough at Killyleagh and what better for the boy than to join the Royal Navy. The only minus point was that none of the Blackwoods had yet joined the Senior Service.

The die was cast. Sir John had a good friend in the navy, Captain John McBride, who hailed from Ballymoney in county Antrim, and he consented to sponsor Henry and keep a fatherly eye on him. It was just as well for Henry enlisted as a child midshipman at the ridiculously innocent age of just 10 years and four months. Boys did join the navy at an early age in those days although they were not supposed to be enlisted until they were 13 years old. It really seemed as if the boy was almost being snatched from his cradle. Life was tough for a 'middie' but for a 10 year old recruit it was likely to be very harsh indeed. Henry doubtless felt scared but was nonetheless determined not to show his emotions to his father.

Why did the Blackwoods send off their youngest, and presumably their mother's dearest, child at such a young age? They certainly would not have had any financial constraints nor was Henry a difficult boy. It just seemed that the time and the inclination were right and off he went.

In 1782 it took two weeks to reach Plymouth from Ireland. The boy left home alone, encumbered by his luggage, trunks and other accoutrements by coach from Ballyleidy for Belfast where he embarked on a small wooden ferryboat which took him to Liverpool. That sea voyage lasted two days and, depending on the state of the sea, could have been either an enjoyable sail or, if the crossing had been rough, a miserable endurance.

Once in England the next days were spent in a variety of coaches and four cramped amongst other passengers who would have had little regard for their young travelling companion. Wayside inns where they found accommodation were notoriously unwelcoming and often downright dangerous. Henry would have been wise enough, however, to keep his head down, both literally and metaphorically. When he was shown to his quarters he would have slept for as many hours as his inebriated fellow travellers would have allowed. Arriving safely at length in Plymouth would have been a triumph in itself. Finding his ship and meeting his captain and his shipmates would have been an altogether different challenge.

Captain McBride, who in his later career went on to become an Admiral, did see that his young charge was received aboard and shown to his corner where he was expected to set out his clothing and prepare for the voyage. No matter how full of resolve and pluck the boy was he did feel homesick and terribly frightened. But he dare not show his emotions especially at this early stage. He put on a brave face and made himself known to those around him. These were the ordinary seamen on this, his first ship, *HMS Artois*. Like all new middies, Henry was, initially at least, rather despised by the hardened crewmen aboard. But he did have other middie companions who were exactly in the same boat, in every sense of the word.

But, apart from the captain, Henry did find a friend who saw to it that he was not overly taunted – one of the ship's gunners. These men were accustomed to this responsibility – they looked after the new midshipmen. Henry was in reasonably good hands and spent these first days on board quietly getting to know the ropes. It was incumbent upon him that he picked up as much knowledge as he could, and as quickly as he could. The more he knew the less he would be teased.

HMS Artois was what was known as a 5th rate frigate of 40 guns. This meant that it was a fast sailing ship, square rigged with three masts and was used for escort and scouting purposes. There were perhaps 10 middies on board, including Henry.

However it was too small a ship to have a schoolmaster of its own and so Captain McBride himself spent time teaching his young charges, not only the aspects of seafaring but also reading and writing. Most of the boys, like Henry, would have had some education before joining up, but there was a great deal more they needed to learn. Every day, whether in port or at sea, the middies attended their school classes. As most of them were literate their progress would have been steady.

The most important lessons were, of course, those pertaining to the sea. They learnt about knots, how to use the sextant and the other navigation devices and it would not have been long before they became useful members of the crews – albeit that some were only 11 or 12 years old. One of the most dangerous tasks a middie had to overcome was climbing up the rigging as far as the very topmast. For a timorous boy who did not have a head for heights, this must have been a complete nightmare. Those boys who were nervous had to do their best to hide their fear for life would have been miserable and they would have been mercilessly bullied. The navy was not the place for a weak boy. But Henry Blackwood survived these ordeals and mastered his nautical skills with ease. This did not mean that he was never subject to degrees of cruelty from older crewmen but he was able to tolerate his taunters.

But there were more terrors for a novice sailor to overcome. On coming on board the *Artois* Henry found himself in fairly squalid accommodation. Gone were the days of ease and pleasure and spacious living at Ballyleidy and Killyleagh. He now found himself in a depressingly dirty and foul smelling mess which was to be his living and sleeping quarters for the duration. His living space was dark, below decks, crowded and only with head height of 5′ 6″. In this small and cramped room he had a table of sorts, and just enough space to put his chest which had to double as a seat.

And then he had his hammock. He had never slept on a hammock before and it took time to master the art of firstly getting up on to it and more importantly how to sleep on it. There was very little space between hammocks, perhaps only 18″ at most, so it was imperative that he mastered hammock drill as quickly as possible. He had joined the navy and had to make the best of it. Henry did, at least, have a 'hammock man' to assist him with his chores and this made life a deal more tolerable. This man was an older sailor whose job it was to take a young middie under his wing and try to help him when he could. It was he who showed Henry where to stow his hammock each morning and how to rotate the two he owned so that one was always clean. This worked well as long as they were not involved in a fight at sea when often all sorts of dispensable objects, including hammocks, were simply thrown overboard.

Although midshipmen were by far the youngest crew members, they were fairly high up the pecking order. Their food, unlike that served to the other crewmen, was of adequate quality and they could always supplement their diet with sweetmeats and other niceties bought when the ship was in port. Captains also ensured that fresh fruit and vegetables were brought on board for all hands when the men were ashore.

However food for the sailors was atrocious and, what's more, insufficient. The only food item in plentiful supply was ships biscuits which were as hard as nails but at least had the advantage of lasting long owing to their toughness. Meat, which had been doused in salt for months, resembled hard wood with a similar consistency. When it was anyway edible it was gristly and fatty. John Masefield, in his book 'Sea Life in Nelson's Time', graphically describes food and drink for the sailors in His Majesty's Navy. 'Pea soup was good; porridge bad; cocoa villainous; scotch coffee (burnt biscuit boiled in water) tolerable and cheese was the most abominable stuff imaginable. Water was also bad and beer, while it lasted, good.'[1]

All that remained to make life bearable was grog, which was spirits mixed with water with some lemon and sugar added. Henry regularly saw the crewmen in various states of inebriation, often too drunk even to stand up. He was quick to understand the misery of life for an ordinary sailor although he could only but wonder why the men were so severely punished for drinking excessively when the officers had sanctioned and even served the grog to the men themselves. It seemed yet another cruel irony of life at sea. He resolved, even in these early days, to ensure that when he had command of a ship himself that he would be a more considerate officer who would treat his men with compassion rather than with cruelty.

Midshipmen needed a private income to survive financially in the navy. This clearly meant that only the sons of well-to-do families could afford to join the service, at least as a potential officer. In his first two or three years Henry was earning the princely sum of £9 per annum and out of this he had to contribute to the cost of his teacher – either the captain or, if he had one at any stage in his education, the schoolmaster. This amount was at least half of his annual pay. It was fortunate that Henry's father was prepared to subsidise his son.

The scene is set

Henry was now settled aboard *HMS Artois*. Like most child midshipmen he was nattily dressed. He wore a blue tail-coat trimmed with silk which sported some fancy buttons. He wore a waistcoat, white breeches and a three cornered hat. His shirt was made of linen and on his feet he wore black shoes. Not all middies were so well dressed but Henry was sufficiently well motivated to present the picture of a youngster ready for duty. This was a wise decision because those of his middie colleagues who chose to dress in a slapdash manner were soon taken to task by the ship's captain.

HMS Artois took up its duties in the English Channel during 1781 and was involved in the drawn battle of Dogger Bank. Henry was not on board in this engagement but it was not long until he experienced an encounter with an enemy ship, the French ship, *Prince de Robego* . Henry was just 12 years old and there he was with guns blazing away in deadly earnest all around him. He saw shipmates severely injured and others killed whilst he hurried about the ship taking messages from one officer to another. Thankfully the action was soon over when the *Artois* got the better of her opponent and the Frenchman surrendered. It was a true baptism of fire for young

Henry and he would have learned much about preserving his life while carrying out his duties in time of battle.

By the time he changed ships in February 1783, Henry was becoming a hardened sailor. He joined *HMS Boreas* which was a smaller 6th rate frigate of 28 guns. Soon the ship was ordered to the West Indies – a journey which lasted many weeks. In the stifling heat of the Caribbean islands with their romantic sounding names – Montserrat, Barbados and St Lucia – Henry could only marvel at the difference in life styles between the islanders and the British seamen.

As he landed on some of these islands he met there the indigenous population with their bright clothes and happy disposition. For a 12 year old boy from Killyleagh to be amongst the black skins of the West Indians and to be partaking of their food and drink and their way of life generally was an experience Henry would never forget.

His stay aboard *Boreas*, as a member of Captain Augustus Montgomery's crew, lasted just seven months. While they were still in the West Indies, Henry was transferred, with his captain, to *HMS Concorde* which was a slightly bigger 5th rate frigate of 36 guns. *Concorde* was a captured French vessel and, like many enemy ships captured by the British navy, it had retained its former name. The ships only stayed in West Indian waters for a short time before being ordered home and, back in England, Henry was discharged. This meant, as it did for any naval officer of whatever rank, that he was unemployed.

Fortunately he was soon enlisted and mustered as a member of the crew of *HMS Druid* which was another 5th rate frigate of about the same size as his previous ship, *HMS Concorde*. Henry was pleased to discover that this ship's captain was none other than Captain John McBride, his early mentor. The kindly Ulsterman was delighted to see the progress his young protégé had made. Young Henry Blackwood was exactly the kind of young middie whom he wanted on board his ship. This time their duties were to sail off the southern Irish coast which were unfamiliar waters for the young Blackwood. His competency was greatly improving and it seemed that the boy was destined to become a sailor of note.

Barely six months later, however, there was another change for Henry. After being discharged from the *Druid*, he was almost immediately mustered as a midshipman on board *HMS Rose*, a smaller 6th rate frigate of 28 guns. For a year he was continuing to learn his trade as the *Rose* patrolled off the Scottish coast. By the time he left this ship it was the middle of 1785. Henry was still only 14 and a half years old and was a seasoned sailor who had already been aboard six separate commands.

Time for reflection

Henry had now been in His Majesty's Navy for over 4 years. He had continued his education under the tutelage of caring captains. He was, by now, proficient in the art of seamanship. He had learned to mix with the men, never getting too friendly with them but still always able to avoid difficult situations. He had experienced the mess with rowdy and drunken sailors and had even tasted grog and spirits himself. He knew that it was incumbent upon him to understand the ordinary sailor yet never to become like one of them.

Henry had known the loneliness of being so far from his home which he had not seen since that April day in 1781 when he had bade farewell to his parents and his brothers and sisters. He did not know when he would ever return although he kept his hopes high in the anticipation of once more seeing the green fields of county Down.

By now he was seasoned midshipman and, like so many other young men with potential, Henry was beginning to assume responsibilities over men aboard ship. It is difficult to imagine a 14 year old giving orders to men perhaps three times his age. But this was becoming the reality. Even when in the West Indies Henry had to ensure that the ship was supplied with fresh water. So he was required to take charge of one of the ship's boats, crew it with sailors, enter the nearest port and arrange for the water vats to be replenished. He had to haggle with the locals who oftentimes made life difficult for visiting crewmen and had to make sure that the task allotted to him was fulfilled to the letter. He never failed his captains who were impressed by Henry's abilities in command.

Henry was a competent sailor. Like others he had to suffer many a rough sea and, like others, he would have been seasick from time to time. This was no shame for even such a great seaman as Admiral Lord Nelson was very often terribly seasick. The lad had mastered the rudiments of navigation and general seamanship. He kept his space clean; he regularly changed and washed his clothes; he attended musters and climbed atop the ship when ordered to do so. He endeavoured to keep within the rules laid down and never had to be unduly punished for any offences. He certainly had never to be top-masted, which entailed a miscreant having to spend upwards of 24 hours on the very top mast of the ship – a dangerous location which led to the deaths of many sailors when they fell into the sea during foul weather.

In a word, Henry Blackwood was proving to be friendly and hard working and yet had the sense to remain just enough of 'one of the lads' as not to be seen as some kind of captain's favourite. A teacher's pet, even in those circumstances and in those days, was not the person to be – even then everyone hated a teacher's pet.

Henry now wanted to become an officer himself and to pass his lieutenant's examinations. So he started to prepare himself for this eventuality although it would still be three or four years before he attained that goal. But he was certainly aiming in the right direction.

A three year stint aboard *HMS Trusty*

In July 1785 Henry Blackwood joined *HMS Trusty*, a 4th rate frigate of 50 guns. This was the largest ship which Henry had sailed on to date. He was to remain on board for over three years and this continuity gave the young, and ever more confident, midshipman many more opportunities to shine. His skills in seamanship were advancing day by day; his leadership of men in the numerous tasks allotted to him was exemplary and his congeniality was admired by officers and sailors alike. His captain certainly had no complaints – quite the contrary — he felt able to entrust the young Henry with more and more responsibilities.

The *Trusty* spent much of her time on station in the Mediterranean. Now Henry had experienced the turbulent seas of the notorious Bay of Biscay and had known the vagaries of passing through the Straits of Gibraltar and into the Mediterranean Sea. The ship called at many of the ports and, to add to the thrill of being a sailor, he had encountered enemy ships some of which the *Trusty* had captured. These were some of the first prize ships which Henry's ship had taken. A prize was doubly important to captains and sailors alike. It showed the skill and prowess of the competency of British seamen but it also brought added income to all on board. When an enemy ship was captured its cargo was impounded and sold back in a British or local friendly port. The money from the prize was divided up and every crewman, from the captain down, or from the lowliest sailor up, was entitled to a share of the booty.

Over the years Henry was to supplement his pay with money from such prizes. Ship's crews, of course, had to ensure that they themselves were never captured for they then would suffer the humiliation of defeat and the surrendering of their own ships and cargoes to the enemy. Fortunately, for Henry, this never happened to him although, as we shall later discover, he was to suffer setbacks, some of considerable magnitude.

These exciting days came to an end in Gibraltar late in 1788. As was so often the case in the precarious life of a British sailor, Henry found himself discharged from HMS *Trusty*, a ship which he had loved, and aboard HMS *Phaeton*, a 5th rate frigate of 38 guns, for a journey back to England. On arrival at Spithead, Henry was rather unceremoniously discharged and unemployed for the second time in his career to date. The country, almost strange to say, was at peace and there was no longer any need for ships and sailors – and even experienced midshipmen – to be on hand for battles with an enemy.

Home again

However Henry was quite happy at this change of circumstance. He had not seen his family and his beloved parents for nearly eight years. He packed his bags, sent a letter home to Ballyleidy announcing his imminent arrival and set out on that tiresome coach journey to Liverpool. This time, at least, he did not have to sit crushed up against some inconsiderate passenger or other. His fine naval attire made him instantly respected by his fellow travellers who were regaled by his stories of life at sea in His Majesty's Navy. He was a popular companion and his stories of life in the West Indies and his exploits in the Mediterranean fairly shortened the long journey through the counties of western England on the way to the sea port of Liverpool.

Henry could not wait for the sea passage from England to Belfast to end. Having attained Irish soil once more, the journey by coach and four to Ballyleidy seemed endless. As the carriage drove up the driveway Henry looked out to see the family standing on the front steps to meet a son and brother who had been away since the early days of his childhood. What a fine sight met their eyes. Lady Dorcas could only wonder at the change in her son. He had left home as a little boy and now he had returned as a fine and handsome young man. His father was equally proud at seeing his youngest boy and Henry's sisters and brothers were delighted to meet a young brother they had wondered if they would ever see again.

Time in county Down seemed to stand still. Henry renewed the acquaintance of his siblings, strode the gardens and rode to hounds once more.

During his stay back home Henry returned to his beloved Killyleagh where he renewed his quayside friendships and sailed the little fishing boats from the town's pier. It was wonderful for him to stay in the castle once again and to savour the relaxed atmosphere of an unrushed life in the idyllic surroundings of the fields and shorelines of county Down.

At Ballyleidy, his favourite sister, Catherine, painted Henry's portrait – a full length study with Henry dressed in his midshipman's uniform. The painting exists to this day.

Sadly it was soon time to return to the south of England. The thought of that tedious journey was only tempered for Henry by the anticipation of at last becoming one of the officer class. After eight years in the navy it was time to sit his lieutenant's examinations. He had studied diligently and, upon arrival back in London, he was summoned by the Lords Commissioners of the Admiralty to attend Somerset House where he was to sit his tests. He satisfied their Lordships proving to them that he could competently navigate a ship, read the weather signs and proficiently use a ship's compass. Above all he showed that he was a sober and serious young man fitted for the responsibilities of an officer.

Following the examination by these worthy men, Henry Blackwood passed their every requirement and became a lieutenant of His Majesty's Navy. The future seemed bright for this young man from county Down. His naval career as an officer and gentleman was assured. All he had to do now was to find a ship and a captain willing to take aboard this eager young lieutenant.

His chance came soon afterwards. Henry was ordered to *HMS Queen Charlotte*, a huge, newly built 1st rate three decker of 100 guns. It was by far the biggest ship Henry had joined and was a prime appointment for him. However he was not taken on as Lieutenant Blackwood. He was to be a Signal Midshipman which post, although not just as prestigious as that of lieutenant, certainly was an important position on such a mighty vessel. This proved to be an excellent opportunity for Henry to show off his skills such as his knowledge of flags signalling and the sending of messages to other ships, so vital in times of conflict.

What of life aboard His Majesty's Ships

HMS Queen Charlotte was, for Henry, his eighth ship in as many years. It was a 1st rate ship whereas his previous ones had been 4th, 5th and 6th rates. The *Queen Charlotte* was a three deck ship with a massive amount of fire power. In the late 17th century British ships were considered inferior in design to French and Spanish ones. They were described as 'cumbrous hulks' and had many defects. They were constructed out of doors in all weathers and consequently many of the navy's newly built ships were already rotting by the time they were launched. Wooden nails were used which, of course, quickly deteriorated and let water in. Some new ships only lasted 8 or 9 years, although some, like Nelson's flagship *HMS Victory*, did remain in service a great deal longer.

Continental ships were roomier; British ships were cramped with too low ceilings. Continental ships were faster; British ships were slow and unwieldy. Continental ships were designed with flair and innovation; British ships were built with too rigid a design. Had it not been for French ships having inferior gun power, then the British navy would have suffered defeat after defeat. But this was the telling factor for the British. Not only were their guns better, but their captains and officers were much more imaginative and heroic. They won battles by surprising their enemies with their unorthodox manoeuvres and audacious attacks.

British ships were, as we have seen, rated according to size and firepower. A 1st rate ship was the biggest (often over 2,000 tons) with the greatest fire power (perhaps with over 100 guns), with a 6th rate being the smallest. There were many other smaller vessels – cutters, schooners, sloops and ketches – and their job was to assist the great, and less manoeuvrable, vessels in battle by delivering messages vital to the effort and also by diverting and harassing the great enemy ships.

The bigger the ship, the more decks it had. A three decker was the leviathan of the navy's ships. It may have needed over 3,000 oak trees from an English forest to construct and it had guns on each of the decks. It was a formidable opponent in the heat of battle. But it wasn't without its disadvantages. The space between the decks was often lower than 5′ 6″ which meant that fighting men, bringing cannon balls and ammunition to the guns, were not able to stand up in that confined and often smoke filled space. The greatest danger, apart from enemy shot actually directly hitting the crew member and carrying off his head, was the hazard of being hit by flying splinters. Many sailors were frightfully injured by shards of wood lodging in all parts of the body. Splinter wounds killed as many men as did direct hits from shot and cannon ball.

There was no conformity as to the colour of these great ships. Blues, reds and yellows were prominent and chosen at the captain's personal whim. Below decks, however, there was consistency. Everywhere was painted red – for very obvious reasons. In times of battle, however, British ships quickly painted their masts white to avoid confusion between the combatants by having the same black coloured masts. It would have been quite a feat for sailors to climb the masts with their white paint pots as the enemy bore down on them. But many lives were saved in life and death struggles by this piece of common sense. No sooner were the seamen back down on deck from their painting task than they were manning the guns to prepare to fire on the enemy ships.

Accommodation on board His Majesty's ships was commensurate with a man's rank. The captain had spacious quarters at the stern of the ship. He had separate rooms for sleeping and dining and, pointedly, had high ceilings in his rooms. Officers lived in their 'cupboards' which were small, yet comfortable rooms near the skipper's section of the ship. The lower the rank meant the further down in the bowels of the ship these men had to live and sleep.

Young midshipmen did not have salubrious quarters. They had to mess below decks where the ceiling height was barely 5′ 6″ and where there pervaded a foul smelling atmosphere. However, although close to the lowest of the low – the ordinary seamen — they did have a small place to call their own for their few possessions and utensils. But the lasting memory of a crowded ship was of rows and rows of hammocks with stinking, drunken men sleeping upon them. Little middies like Henry grew up very quickly in the navy. There was nothing else for it. No one was going to listen to their complaints. They knew their place in the scheme of things and they could but look to the day when promotion would remove them from their filthy surroundings.

2.
When Henry Almost Lost His Life

In April 1791, still aged only 20 yet with almost ten years of service under his belt, Henry finally got his big chance. He was appointed as 3rd lieutenant on *HMS Proserpine*, a mere 6th rate frigate of 28 guns. He had hoped for a higher rank and an even larger ship but he was pleased to have attained the higher rank at long last. He spent his few months on this ship as part of the Channel fleet but, before he knew it, he was once more discharged towards the end of that year. There was no war and the ship was not needed at sea on patrol. Lieutenant Henry Blackwood was once more surplus to requirements in his naval career.

Revolutionary France

As soon as Henry collected his pay he made up his mind not to return on holiday to county Down but to proceed to France. He was keen to learn the language. This was a commendable aspiration had it not been for the fact that the bloody French revolution was barely two years old. Life in that country was decidedly unstable.

At the outset he headed for Angouleme, a town in western France north of the city of Bordeaux. He studied French and could soon speak as well as any Englishman. He now sought adventure – for that must have been his reason for leaving the safety of Angouleme to travel to the French capital. Revolution was still very much in the air. The revolutionaries were fighting amongst themselves and Paris was a dangerous place to be – especially for a foreigner.

Not only did Henry decide to go there, regardless of the terror, but he agreed to carry a small book to the city for émigré friends of his. This was an unwise decision to say the least. On arrival in Paris, swarming as it was with criminals and rebels, he was arrested and found to have the damning evidence of this book on his person. He was thrown into jail and threatened with the fate of all those who opposed the Republic – Madame la Guillotine. Had it not been for a remarkably good, and it must be said brave, French friend who vouched for Henry, his head surely would have gone the way of thousands before him – into the basket beneath the guillotine. But although there was a shouting match between the exasperated prosecutor and M. Lafitteau, Henry's saviour, he was released. Henry took the first available coach to the Channel ports to return to England thanking his lucky stars – and M. Lafitteau.

Henry immediately made it known that he was available for duty to the Lords Commissioners and was pleased to be appointed as second lieutenant of *HMS Invincible* – a 3rd rate 74 gun ship of the line. (He is listed as having been a crew member of *HMS Active* some time before he boarded *Invincible* but the exact dates have not been accurately recorded. However it seems almost certain that he did have about 6 weeks aboard *Active*).

A first real taste of battle

Henry had returned, suitably chastened from his French escapade, at the end of September 1792, but he was still unemployed. His appointment to *Invincible* did not take effect until mid 1793 and, in the meantime, he had time on his hands. In all likelihood he did return to Ireland, reacquainting himself with his old haunts around Bangor and in Killyleagh.

Eventually Henry took up his position as second lieutenant aboard *Invincible*. The promotion was welcomed both by Henry himself and also by his friends and family. He was becoming popular with the ordinary crewmen too. His star was in the ascendant.

With Britain again at war with France, *Invincible* took to patrolling the English Channel and Henry learned the importance of vigilance. It was a vital job to ensure that no enemy ship got through their blockade where it could so easily have spied on British dockyards and ports.

Henry's next big chance came the following year. In 1793, having only been on *Invincible* for a few months, Henry was further advanced to first lieutenant. He was now on the verge of real power for if, for any reason, his captain was killed, injured or otherwise incapacitated, then he would be expected to take command of the ship. It also meant that, whilst effectively running the ship, the first lieutenant did the work while the captain took the plaudits and the glory. And soon he was to have his first taste of battle; of death and destruction; of blood and gore.

In the last days of May 1794 the British fleet, under Admiral Lord Howe, with 26 ships, including Henry's, engaged the French fleet with approximately the same number of ships nearly 500 miles off the French port of Ushant in the Atlantic Ocean. The battle was a protracted affair with the opposing fleets carefully sounding each other out. On the so-called Glorious First of June, Admiral Howe, aboard Henry's old ship *HMS Queen Charlotte*, tore into the French. Like all British admirals and captains, he had singled out his opponent and driven almost recklessly into that unfortunate ship before it realised what had hit it.

In the battle which ensued Henry's ship was out of action for some time owing to problems with its masts. However, when Admiral Howe had forced the French to surrender after a truly bloody encounter, Henry was ordered to take one of his boats from *Invincible* and board the French ship, *Le Juste*, to take its surrender. This he successfully completed, although Henry had to thwart the injured French captain from deliberately blowing up his ship and prevent its being taken as a prize.

Henry was commended for his bravery in action and for taking the *Le Juste* in tow. Admiral Howe's flagship, *HMS Queen Charlotte*, had borne the brunt of heavy enemy fire and was virtually crippled. Its masts had been blown away and her decks littered with the detritus of battle. He then came aboard *Invincible* which he made his new flagship and returned to England in triumph.

The *Invincible* brought its prize, the *Le Juste*, into Portsmouth harbour to the cheers and acclaim of a thankful population. Once more the British fleet had triumphed although it too had suffered damage and many losses. Henry, in taking stock of his crew after the battle, was saddened to find that over 40 of his men had been killed or injured. No victory was ever claimed without loss of life on the victor's side. He had seen for himself the horrendous injuries caused by splinters and cannon balls for the first time. He had experienced the trauma of assisting his badly mauled men below deck where they were treated by the ship's surgeons. He had seen his friends die in unspeakable circumstances. It had not been a pretty sight but, now as a senior naval officer, he knew the significance of that fine line which separates life from death.

After the battle and the safe arrival in port of the battered fleet and its prizes, King George III showed his appreciation by holding a levee at which he honoured the victors of this sea battle. The most senior men were given titles and presented with gold swords and Henry too was exceedingly pleased at his recognition. He was promoted to the rank of commander. He was now a ship's captain, provided a ship became available.

It was the late summer of 1794 and Henry Blackwood was just 23 years old. After 13 years, more than half his life, he had attained this very prestigious rank. He was rightly proud of himself. He pondered on the future and, whilst in this reverie, there came word from the Lords Commissioners. Captain Henry Blackwood had been allocated to his first command – *HMS Magaera*.

3.
Master and Commander

When Henry realised that the *Magaera* was a fire ship, he almost had second thoughts about the offer made to him. Fire ships were small; they needed relatively few crewmen (55) and they were built for a rather disagreeable purpose. They were built to a basic design with large holds which could quickly and easily be filled with combustible material and explosives. When in action, thus ladened, they were sailed against the side of a much larger enemy ship, preferably unseen by that enemy vessel, and then set on fire. These were the archetypal dispensable warships. Cheaply built with very few embellishments, they were to act as floating bombs. They would, therefore, only have lasted until their first operation. After that they were, of course, utterly destroyed.

For the first time in his career Henry realised how difficult it was to man a ship. Imagine his even greater problems in trying to man a fire ship. It may only have required 55 men but it took Captain Blackwood an incredibly long time to find his crew. At length he did, mainly by pressing men from the local ports, and the ship set out. Henry was *Magaera's* commander for just 10 months and, fortunately for himself and his crew, his little ship was never called upon to undertake the task for which it had been built. Consequently, and even more providentially, neither he nor his crew had to fling themselves into the sea before impact when their only hope of survival would have been to be rescued by other friendly ships or make their escape on the ship's boats which had been towed astern their ship. As far as the Royal Navy was concerned there could hardly have been a more unsavoury posting for either captain, officer or crew member. Henry's only consolation would have been a financial one – as captain of the *Magaera* he earned £109 per annum as opposed to his £73 as a first lieutenant aboard *Invincible*.

Marriage

At the end of December 1794, some months after taking command of the *Magaera,* Henry took leave. Early in January 1795 he married Jane Mary Crosbie who hailed from county Kerry in the south west of Ireland. At first glance it is hard to imagine when Henry could have met his future wife. However there are some clues.

The Blackwoods, to begin with, owned land in county Kerry. Jane Mary's father was an MP and, as Henry's father was MP for Killyleagh at that time, it is certain these men would have been acquainted with one another. The families would have perhaps visited each other, although it was a long way from county Down to county Kerry. Consequently Jane Mary would have been in the company and would have met Henry when he visited home after his disastrous sojourn in France. Be that speculation as may be, the young couple married in Portsmouth and set up a home in Hampshire. There was no honeymoon as such as Henry was urgently required to return to the *Magaera.* Like so many naval captains and their crews, the men saw very little of their wives. Taking into account the fact that voyages often lasted for years on end, it seems an dreadful imposition on the womenfolk who had to wait interminably for their husbands to come home. It was no life for the children of sailors; they hardly knew their fathers at all.

Post Captain Henry Blackwood

Henry must have pleased their Lordships with his devotion to *HMS Magaera* for, in less than a year, he received the welcome news that, not only was he leaving the *Magaera,* but he was to be further promoted to Post Captain with his reward the captaincy of the 2 deck, 64 gun ship of the line, *HMS Nonsuch.* There was a subtle difference between being a Post Captain and a mere captain. Post Captains alone were eligible to move up the promotion ladder as far as the giddy heights of Rear Admiral and even Admiral. By becoming Post Captain of the *Nonsuch*

Henry, now just 24 years old, had taken the first important step towards naval greatness. Whether he would fulfil these great expectations in due course would be for him to aspire to and for others to decide. But, putting these aspirations aside, he could see an immediate advantage upon his promotion – his pay had more than doubled to £226 per annum.

A dinky, dapper sailor

It is amusing to note that Henry Blackwood, an otherwise kindly, sober and considerate man and a loving husband, was also a very vain man. Throughout his life he had two consuming passions – looking the part as a senior personage in His Majesty's Navy and keeping himself in trim.

In pursuit of the former intention, Henry became a regular and valued customer of Mr Lock who owned the famous hatters' shop in St James' Street in the city of London. On almost every visit ashore he made his way to see Mr Lock and to buy from him various styles of hats – tall ones, Bedford ones, silk ones and all manner of natty headgear. He also made a point of ensuring that he was seen wearing all his new and fashionable hats as he strode about the streets of the metropolis.

As far as his latter passion of watching his figure was concerned Henry, often after purchasing a new hat, made tracks for Berry's, the wine merchants, further down St James' Street – not to buy wine but to have himself weighed. Berry's was one of the few shops which had a pair of scales and it was on their weighbridge that Henry checked his weight throughout his entire naval career. For a 'rather short, well set up, stocky in build, with a ruddy face'[2] kind of man, Henry's average 13 stone frame might seem, in today's parlance at any rate, a trifle heavy. His weight rarely fluctuated over many years and this doubtless would have pleased Henry.

A rather disappointing ship of the line

It was a classic case of good news, bad news. The good news was the fact that Henry Blackwood had been promoted to Post Captain at the early age of 24. The bad news, however, was that *HMS Nonsuch* must have been the ship in the poorest shape in all His Majesty's fleet. Even though it was a 3rd rate the ship was nothing better than a floating hulk. It was already over 20 years old and had seen lots of service. It was badly in need of attention and, when Henry first set his eyes on his new command, his heart sank. Despite writing voluminously to the Lords Commissioners about the urgent work required on his ship, very few of their responses satisfied Captain Blackwood. And what was more, *Nonsuch* was to undertake the degrading job of acting as a guard ship to be used to keep enemy ships out of the river Humber on the east coast of England.

And then there was the perennial problem of manning the ship. If it was difficult to find men for his fire ship, *Magaera*, it was nothing compared with crewing the *Nonsuch*. In effect the ship's name said it all. For months he struggled to seek out pressed men, more often than not the dregs of society, and track down men who had deserted their posts. Dealing with deserters was a constant problem for ships' captains and all the more so for Henry who did not even have a decent ship for them to join.

He approached the Lord Mayor in the hope that the city Corporation would find crewmen for the *Nonsuch*. Many towns and cities at that time had responsibilities to find a quota of men for the navy and so Hull was being asked to help the *Nonsuch*. Henry found himself in hot water with the Lord Mayor of Hull who had complained to the Lords Commissioners about Henry's attitude to him. As with every dispute involving the Admiralty the matter took ages to resolve but, in due course, Henry was exonerated.

Being the captain of such a vessel as the *Nonsuch* brought Henry no relief at all. It was the constant trial of trying to crew the ship and to deal with haughty town officials. Even when they did get into the North Sea the task allotted was boring and unrewarding. He was delighted and thankful, then, to receive the news, early in May 1796, that he was to be chosen for another command – *HMS Brilliant* — which was a much newer and active frigate. The down side was that it was just a 6th rate ship and immediately Henry suffered a cut in salary of almost £100 per annum. But he did not care. The *Brilliant* was a fine ship and, as it was on active service, there would be every expectation of taking prizes and thus supplementing his income. And to add to his sense of relief, the ship was already crewed and was sailing to Hull to collect him. Ships' captains were always permitted to take a small quota of crewmen from their former commands aboard their new ones and so Henry chose his most able men and brought them with him to *Brilliant*.

The *Brilliant* was soon ready for sea and for many months Henry and his crew sailed the waters of the North Sea and the Baltic keeping an eye on the sea lanes and ensuring that any potential enemy ships were beaten off. The presence of the *Brilliant*, in itself, served the purpose. No one would want to challenge Henry Blackwood's and *HMS Brilliant's* authority. When an opportunity arose for their little frigate to pounce on a suspicious ship the chance was never squandered. Such regular quarry enabled the *Brilliant's* coffers to be replenished. Prizes meant extra money and further prestige for the ship's captain and crew.

Prizes and mutinies

The prospect of taking prizes was always an attractive one. Not only were the rewards worthwhile for both captain and crew alike, but the reputations gained thereby gave many commanders an aura of invincibility. To have such a reputation also gave British sea captains a certain kudos. *Brilliant* was such a ship and Henry Blackwood became such a commander.

Captains, however, had to be extremely careful about capturing prizes. A legitimate prize was a ship whose manifest did not tally with what the boarding party found in the ship's hold. If a seemingly neutral ship was discovered to be carrying weapons to Cadiz and not the oranges to a Mediterranean port as per its manifest then the ship was asking to be captured. The ship would be taken in tow and brought to a British port.

But there always was a down side for the ever vigilant seafaring British naval personnel. They occasionally made the wrong decision and accused an innocent skipper of carrying counterfeit goods only to discover that was not the case. Then complaints were directed at the Admiralty and overly zealous captains were hauled over the coals. This did happen to Henry on one or two occasions but, fortunately for him, he was always absolved from blame at the subsequent hearing. The watchword, therefore, was caution.

A very significant event in British naval history took effect on 16 April 1797 at the Spithead base. A mutiny broke out when a large number of sailors refused to put to sea when ordered to do so. They were demanding improvements for the lot of British sailors. In retrospect their demands were perfectly legitimate – better pay, better provisions and improved conditions. They were poorly paid and catered for and it might have been thought that the Admiralty would have had some sympathy with their men. The Lords Commissioners did make amends after an Act of Parliament had been passed to show the government's good intent. The mutiny soon ended.

But just as the Spithead men were returning to their duties, their colleagues at the Nore struck too. They made more demands including a bigger share of the booty from prizes. This mutiny not only turned more ugly but it also directly involved Henry.

His ship was at the Nore being repaired when its crew joined the mutineers and he was totally chagrined when some of his own men took over the *Brilliant* and kept Henry as a virtual prisoner for over a month. It was an ignominious position to find himself in but he proved to be a patient man and sat out the period of forced imprisonment. Interestingly, yet not surprisingly, Henry agreed with many of the demands of his men. He had always been a champion of the underpaid and overworked British sailor; he had himself brought changes to better the lot of these men; he understood their travails.

However he could also see the position of the navy. A country could not have its navy inoperative in time of war or in time of a threat of conflict. So, when the mutiny finally ended, Henry acquiesced in the execution of the ringleaders. To his credit Henry had appeared on behalf of a couple of the leaders, but they were, in the end, put to death. Of the men on his own ship who mutinied, 11 were court-martialled. They were severely punished but none were executed. It was a mark of Henry Blackwood, the caring and considerate master and commander of men.

Continuing difficult times for Henry Blackwood

The mutiny at the Nore, having now been resolved, brought Henry back to the daily round of captaincy of the *Brilliant*. The ship had never been in very good shape although its recent repairs had enabled it to continue on its assigned tasks. Duties during the latter part of 1797 saw the ship sailing the waters off the east of Great Britain – patrolling the east Scottish coast as far north as Aberdeen and ensuring the safety of British merchant ships off the east coast of England. This was not exactly a glamorous assignment but Henry did at least have the satisfaction that his men were gainfully employed following the disruptions of the Nore mutiny. And he also sympathised with his colleagues on other ships many of whose sailors had been put to death after the mutiny. A busy life at sea certainly took their minds off these more maudlin thoughts.

Sadness once more overtook Henry Blackwood. At just 27 and after only 3 years of marriage, he found himself a widower. He had been urgently called to his wife's side early in January 1798 to discover, too late, that Jane Mary had already died. As is too often the case the circumstances of her death remained unknown. He only knew that he had lost a dear wife with whom, as a sea captain, he had spent too short a time. Jane Mary may have died of some virulent disease that was prevalent at the time or simply had been unfortunate to succumb to some relatively trivial sickness which today would have been treated in an instant.

Life at sea did mean that he had little time to mourn. He was required to take *Brilliant* to Irish waters and then to the other side of the Atlantic – to Newfoundland. Having unsuccessfully tried to arrest ships as prizes Henry did, at last, make a lucrative capture of a Spanish ship and was able to reap his reward in due course. There were occasions when, during his career in the navy, Henry did greatly benefit from the income of his prizes. A year or two after this particular capture he received over £6,000 (£700,000 in today's money) as his portion of a prize. It would only have taken one such prize to make a sea captain a wealthy man for life. It surely did give Henry a firm footing on the stepladder to fame and fortune.

The fear, or the thrill, of combat with the enemy is uppermost in the mind of all sailors and more so, naturally, for ships' captains. To date Henry had not had to test his mettle in such a circumstance. But, at the end of July 1798, as *Brilliant* was returning from the Newfoundland station, his little 28 gun frigate was most certainly called upon to show her prowess and the skills of its captain in a fight. Off the Azores islands *Brilliant* was run down by two French 36 (or perhaps 44) gun frigates which gave immediate chase. It looked a certain victory for the Frenchmen as they started to fire on the lonesome *Brilliant*. But Henry and his crew were determined otherwise and took the fight to the French. In the encounter which ensued, Henry came out on top.

The main reason for his victory was the fact that he took his ship straight into the French ships rather than circling as was the method of the enemy. This allowed *Brilliant* to fire off broadsides against the French frigates and cause early, and very severe, damage. At the end of the engagement the French ships were seriously damaged with many casualties whilst the *Brilliant* came off much better with only few of her men injured.

Victory had been sweet for Henry and his men. Superior enemy firepower had been successfully neutralised. Henry's exploits were mentioned in despatches with a particular commendation for Henry's bravery from Admiral Lord St Vincent himself. Henry Blackwood, no longer captain of fire ship or guard ship, was now in command of an effective fighting ship of the line.

When he returned to port Henry received word of his promotion to *HMS Penelope*, a 5th rate of 36 guns. It was an almost new vessel. Henry was rightly proud of his latest achievement. His advance continued.

HMS Penelope and remarriage

As ever the manning of his new ship proved to be difficult. As captain Henry requested the transfer of a number of his last ship's crew to join him aboard the *Penelope*. The Lords of the Admiralty, as usual, proved inflexible and stalled many of Henry's perfectly legitimate requests. But Henry, as tenacious as always, kept up his lengthy correspondence with London and eventually was able to man his new ship to his satisfaction. During the early months of 1799 the *Penelope* sailed in the English Channel before returning to port.

Henry had applied for leave in May. He had met a lovely young woman, Elizabeth Waghorn, who was the daughter of another naval officer, the late captain Martin Waghorn. Elizabeth was a minor and may have been as young as 17. Where Henry met Elizabeth is uncertain but it could well have been at some naval gathering. The couple were married in London before going off on their honeymoon. Henry was able to spend a little longer with his new wife as the *Penelope* was at sea.

When his family back in county Down heard of their son's betrothal is in doubt but they were represented at the wedding by Sir George Dallas who was married to Henry's sister, Catherine. Henry's father, Sir John, had died earlier in February of 1799 in his 77th year so it is unlikely that Lady Dorcas, his mother, would have attended her youngest son's wedding. The people of Killyleagh would have been pleased to hear that

Henry had remarried and his friends in the village would have sent their congratulations.

All too soon Henry's slightly extended leave was over and he had to bid an early farewell to Elizabeth. *Penelope* had been ordered to the Mediterranean station which, for all sailors, meant an inordinate period of absence from home. Sometimes this tour of duty lasted as long as three years. For Henry it was to be such a long journey and one which was to end in further heartache.

The *Penelope* set sail for Gibraltar and thence into the Mediterranean Sea. Henry was now under the command of Horatio, Lord Nelson and their friendship was to last until Nelson's death at Trafalgar. There was always one distinct advantage in being sent to this part of the world. There were lots of prizes to be had and Henry captured his fair share of them. Arresting ships was always fraught with danger and Henry's crewmen had to be careful as they boarded suspicious vessels. But these French and Spanish privateers were ripe for the picking and the *Penelope* took every opportunity to make extra money from the ships captured. And just as importantly, they were able to glean lots of intelligence concerning the joint enemy fleets from the captains of the captured vessels. Nelson was soon to regard Henry Blackwood as one of his most efficient and vigilant officers.

Henry's finest hour

In the early part of 1800 Lord Nelson had scored one of his greatest victories at the battle of the Nile when he had tracked the enemy fleet into the eastern Mediterranean. His victory had been almost faultless and his preferred method of attacking one ship at a time, taking their surprised surrender and moving on immediately to another target had brought the Admiral great renown. However the remnant of the French fleet had taken refuge in Valetta harbour in the island of Malta. Henry had been ordered to shadow these ships and ensure that they did not escape to their home French ports. The largest of the French ships, the 80 gun *Guillaume (William) Tell* was the ship to watch; it could not be let escape; the blockade must be successful.

On the night of 30 March 1800, *Penelope's* lookouts noticed in the gloom, a huge hulk sailing past them. They gave chase and discovered the ship to be the *Guillaume Tell*. It was a difficult enough task for a little 36 gun frigate to keep a huge 80 gun vessel under surveillance: it was even more dangerous to attack it. But Henry was determined to stop the enemy ship's progress to probable rehabilitation in its home port.

He watched the *Tell* 'as a committee of cats might watch a cornered rat'.[3] Henry summoned help from other British ships and immediately carried out his intention to attack. Had the *Tell* got broadside of the *Penelope* this would have spelt disaster. But Henry cleverly sailed astern of the great French ship thus ensuring that only the enemy's rear guns could be trained on the *Penelope*. This tactic worked perfectly and, before long, the great ship's main masts were blown away and it soon became disabled. The mighty vessel was a complete wreck, such was the expert fire upon her by the *Penelope*. There was severe loss of life aboard the *Guillaume Tell* and, sadly, also amongst the crews of the supporting British ships.

For Henry and his crew the outcome was more satisfactory and deaths amongst his own men were kept to a minimum – there were just three of his men killed and a number wounded. The *Penelope* did suffer some structural damage but Henry was able to report the surrender of the French admiral who was himself injured in the encounter.

Above all, and despite a bout of illness and depression, Lord Nelson was delighted at the outcome. It was at this juncture that he wrote his famous letter to Henry, part of which contained the immortal words – 'My Dear Blackwood, is there a sympathy which ties men together in the bonds of friendship without having a personal knowledge of each other? If so (and, I believe, it was so to you) I was your friend and acquaintance before I saw you.'[4] In fact Nelson had almost certainly been in Henry's company before then but it may have been Nelson's over-dramatic way of saying how pleased he was with such a courageous and diligent captain. Whatever the reason Henry did remain a firm associate and companion of Nelson's for the remainder of the admiral's life. Most surely this was Henry Blackwood's finest hour.

Henry was particularly pleased to receive, from the King of the Two Sicilies, the Grand Sicilian Order of St Ferdinand. He made a plea to King George to be permitted to wear this foreign decoration and was delighted to hear that His Majesty had approved his request. For the rest of his life, Henry wore this sumptuous sash and star whenever a suitable occasion presented itself. From his own sovereign he received the Navy Medal – a fine reward but not quite as splendid as his Sicilian one.

His annus mirabilis was further enhanced when he heard of the birth of his first child, a son, Henry Martin, on 11 June 1800. It was to be, however, a long delay before he set eyes on his son and heir.

After its strenuous efforts in battle, the *Penelope* was back on her routine escort and guard duties in the Mediterranean along the Spanish and Portuguese coasts. Henry continued to consider the circumstances of his men and was always solicitous in seeing that their conditions were as good as could be afforded. His constant correspondence with the Lords of the Admiralty showed just what a fine and reasonable captain he was. Nothing was too much trouble for Henry Blackwood when it came to looking after his men. They had, after all, been away from their homes for well over two years – as, of course, had Henry himself.

There continued to be close contact between Lord Nelson and Henry. They were captains of the same ilk – they liked to see things done unlike their overall commander at the time, Lord Keith. And, from time to time, both men crossed swords with this intransigent admiral.

At long last *Penelope* received orders to return to England and by March 1802 they were back in their homeland. It seems likely that Henry, for some unexplained reason, did not go immediately to see his wife and two year old son. Legal business in the Irish courts took him back to Dublin but the exact details of the need for this visit have not been discovered. He could well have come to his county Down homes at Ballyleidy and Killyleagh during this time. Although there is a vast array of Blackwood papers in existence it is nonetheless disappointing to discover gaps in his movements, such as those relating to his movements and activities when he did return to Ireland. But, being the kind of man he was, he almost assuredly came home to see his aging mother.

Much is made of Henry's regular visits to Lock's for new hats and to Berry's to be weighed and he even appears to have made these calls before going down to his home in Hampshire. When he eventually arrived there in June 1802 he attended the baptism of his son who was, by now, over two years old. Again the exact details of the ceremony and who attended it are vague.

It may be that Elizabeth was absent. She must have been ill for, on 30 October 1802, further tragedy struck poor Henry. Elizabeth, who was hardly 20 years old, died on that day after what was described as a 'lingering illness'. For the second time in a few years the 32 year old Henry Blackwood was a widower once more. He had scarcely seen his second wife having been at sea for the majority of their marriage. Life seemed to the unfortunate Henry to be little more than a lottery as, sadly, it must have been for many in His Majesty's Navy. Henry mourned once more and thought of a life that might have been. He now had a young son who had no mother and he himself was about to become the captain of yet another ship. He had been unemployed, in consequence on half pay, for some months so a new command was welcomed.

Within six months of Elizabeth's death, Henry had married for a third time. In May 1803 his marriage to Harriet Gore took place in Sussex. Harriet may have been little Henry Martin's nanny or governess and was 36 years old, three years Henry's senior. Once more those gaps in Henry's life appear and it is not certain exactly how the couple met. However Harriet seemed to know Henry's son and readily took on the upbringing of the little boy who had lost his own mother at such an early age.

Harriet may have been a nanny but she had worthy antecedents – her late father had once been the Governor of Grenada and the Lieutenant Governor of the West Indies. But, as ever, Henry had to leave his new wife not long after their honeymoon and proceed to Portsmouth where the new 5th rate of 36 guns, *HMS Euryalus,* awaited her new captain. He was to be her skipper for some three years including distinguished service during that epic struggle – the battle of Trafalgar.

4.
Killyleagh at Trafalgar

Euryalus was a new ship and not long launched when Henry took command in June 1803. Although it was a 5th rate 36 gun frigate the ship actually had 42 guns. There were six additional smaller guns aboard making it a sleek fighting machine. This was the first British ship to be named *Euryalus* but many other equally illustrious vessels of the same name have flown the British flag since then. The ship's complement was over 250 men and, after almost three months, Captain Blackwood had *Euryalus* fully manned.

He was particularly pleased that he had been given permission to take a schoolmaster on board. Now his eager young middies would have a first class education from a man who was dedicated to the cause. In some ways he was surprised that the haughty Lords at the Admiralty had granted this request from a captain who had become a thorn in their flesh. New vessels were notoriously tricky to man and Henry spent many nugatory hours over the years cajoling these men to release staff for his commands. He continued to get into trouble for his insolent letters but he kept up the barrage because he believed that His Majesty's frigates should have a crew worthy of his great navy.

The *Euryalus* set sail for Irish waters at the end of August 1803, heading first for Dublin and thence to Cork. Henry landed at Dublin to assist one of his crew members in a personal matter but had not the time to go north and visit his family. Travelling from Dublin to county Down in the early years of the 19th century was a tedious affair which took a great deal of time.

As the ship was approaching the city of Cork its residents noticed something very strange and untoward. At the entrance to the harbour they saw, to their amazement, a fine new ship aground. It was the *Euryalus*. For four days Henry, much to his great embarrassment, had to spend time getting his ship off the sandbank and afloat again. In due time he succeeded but he was teased unmercifully for his poor navigation skills at entering a very straightforward anchorage. It had been an inauspicious start for *Euryalus*. But Henry could take it and proceeded on his journey patrolling the Irish and English channels.

Not for the first, nor for that matter the last, time in his long naval career Henry became so frustrated at his chain of command that he considered resigning. He had the misfortune, once more, to be under the command of Admiral Lord Keith. This straight-laced Scotsman persistently disapproved of Henry's inventive style of captaincy. He baulked at many reasonable requests and stymied Henry's imagination.

At this stage in his career, however, Henry began to make some very influential friends. One of these was none other than the Prime Minister himself, Henry Addington. The premier was able to loosen some of the knots tied by Admiral Keith and soon Henry made progress – to Keith's obvious displeasure. This friendship with Addington (later Lord Sidmouth) was to last throughout Henry's life.

Napoleon Bonaparte

Across the channel in revolutionary France Bonaparte was flexing his muscles. An ambitious and megalomaniacal young man, Napoleon had his eyes firmly set on England with a view to invasion. So he was gathering many of his warships in French ports facing the south coast of England. Henry Blackwood and *Euryalus* were now given the responsible task of monitoring the movements of these enemy ships and sailed up and down the English Channel for months. During this time many prizes were captured. Many were American ships bringing supplies for the French which fell foul of *Euryalus*. This became a lucrative time for Henry and his men.

But the biggest threat was from the Frenchman, Bonaparte. Britain and France were continually on the verge of, or actually in the midst of, a war. By 1804 the countries were hanging over the precipice once more. It would not be long before they were at each other's throats yet again.

Henry sought leave in the middle of 1804. Once more the reasons for this request were as tantalisingly vague as ever. The records of his private life seem to be much less available than those for his naval service. The leave was to be for three weeks but it was extended twice making a total of seven weeks. We do know that Harriet, his wife, was ill around that time and it may well have been to assist her that Henry took his leave. This is, of course, only speculation but, in the circumstances, it was cheering to note that he did have plenty of time at home with Harriet and little Henry, now aged four.

Upon his return to *Euryalus* (which had a temporary captain in his absence) Henry continued on his English Channel duties right through until the middle of 1805. By now the dogs of war were facing the island nation and Henry's vigilance was critical in monitoring the French fleet.

The sea battle to end all sea battles was imminent. Before long the sinews of every British sailor, from crewman up to admiral, were to be severely stretched and tested. And the name of that battle – Trafalgar.

Preparations aboard ship before battle

It cannot be emphasised too strongly how harsh and cruel life aboard a ship of the line, such as *Euryalus*, could be. Although the majority of captains like Henry Blackwood were reasonable and considerate, nonetheless life was dreadful for the ordinary sailors. They lived in stinking, foul-smelling hell holes. The spaces they occupied were badly lit, poorly ventilated and wretched. This was rarely the fault of the men themselves, but more to do with the design of the vessels they sailed. Good captains, like Henry, made sure that sleeping areas and mess rooms were regularly cleaned and kept clear of rubbish and other debris. It was not always an easy or straightforward task.

Disease lurked below deck. Scurvy was the curse of the sailor, mainly caused by lack of vitamin C and by rotten food. Death came suddenly and often inexplicably to men who had been sound and healthy perhaps just a day or two before.

The ship's surgeon was, therefore, a crucial member of the ship's company. However he was never well paid and had only rudimentary instruments with which to treat injuries and maladies. To make matters worse, he usually had to bring his own tools of his trade. The Navy Board did not deem it necessary to provide scalpels, forceps and the like for the doctors who were employed to save life and limb in the heat of battle. Men who were sick were summoned to the surgeon's quarters each day and were treated as required. Their dressings were changed and rudimentary medicines were dispensed.

The 'nurses' in the sick bay, which was at least a clean and comfortable place, were the least skilful sailors called 'waisters'. Many a crewman was kept alive by these underrated and lowly men. These were the men, too, who assisted the surgeons during a struggle at sea when amputations were commonplace. The 'waisters' carried away the severed limbs and mopped up the rivers of blood swilling around in the bowels of the ship. Theirs was surely the most unenviable job aboard ship; theirs is the unsung story of bravery and dedication in the face of adversity, in its starkest possible image.

Weaponry

The archetypal picture of a fighting man o'war in the King's Navy in the 18th century was of a splendid wooden warship sailing over unruffled seas with its sparkling cannons poking out from the ship's sides. The reality, however, was very different – especially in battle. For the crew aboard a ship such as *HMS Euryalus* life was extremely harsh. The men may have been at sea for months on end and never able to spend their meagre pay at foreign or even home ports. They were often hungry, exhausted and miserable. Their lot was rarely a happy one. The approach of an enemy ship, therefore, sent shivers down the spines of the men. They knew that, despite the privations which they had been enduring, they were now expected to fight for the honour of their ship and country and, what was infinitely more urgent, to protect their own lives. They could be dead in a matter of moments if they were not prepared and ready for a fight to the end.

Weaponry aboard ship was, therefore, of the greatest importance. The crew had continually cleaned and polished the cannons; they had checked the stores of ammunition; they had carried out their battle drills. When the conflict erupted they had to be organised.

The most visible and significant weapons on board were the cannons. But there is much more to long-barrelled cannons than meets the eye. These huge brass or iron guns weighed up to 2 tons and took between 4 and 8 men to operate them. They fired cannonballs of between 6 and 32 pounds in weight. Correctly used they wreaked the most awful havoc aboard an enemy ship especially when they were attacking broadsides. But they could be, and often were, even more dangerous to the men whose job it was to load and fire them. The cannons could come off their carriages and career over the deck causing mayhem and sudden death to those unfortunate enough to find themselves in their path. If the gunpowder, brought up from the armoury by the young midshipmen, sweating under the strain, was in any way wet or faulty, this could mean yet more death and injury to the gunners if the cannon misfired. The picture of these brave and brawny men firing their sleek cannons at the enemy may appear idyllic; the reality was quite the opposite. It was a very dangerous occupation to be a ship's gunner especially, of course, in the heat of battle.

There were other weapons which could also cause terrible damage. Cannonades were small guns which fired small cannonballs totally indiscriminately at the enemy ships. Grape and sling shot were absolutely lethal missiles. Imagine all manner of steel items being fired out of a red-hot cannon and bursting through a line of your friends and shipmates, cutting them to ribbons. Very often, too, it was your turn next. In truth it was a mercy for such injured men to die instantly rather than surviving to suffer amputation and ghastly wounds. When the crewmen eventually got the order to board the enemy ship, then a man's musket, cutlass, pistol, pike or even his tomahawk was his sole protection between life and death. Nothing could ever prepare us today for the utter devastation and downright and abject horrors of what it was just to save one's own life in circumstances we cannot possibly imagine.

And thus it was that the great sea battle of Trafalgar loomed. By the end of October 1805 life in Europe had changed for ever. Henry Blackwood, Killyleagh born and county Down bred, now prepared to take his part in this heroic struggle.

Blackwood watches while Nelson waits — the prelude to the Battle of Trafalgar

At the beginning of August 1805, whilst still cruising the waters around the south of Ireland, Henry received urgent orders to break off these duties and to proceed to the coast of Portugal and report directly to Admiral Lord Nelson on the position of the combined enemy fleet.

An abortive action between the French and Admiral Sir Robert Calder had recently taken place off Ferrol in northern Spain. The Lords of the Admiralty had shown their displeasure at Calder for not having been more decisive and carried victory for the British fleet. However they needed to know exactly what the French intended to do, whether they would sail north into the English Channel or south back to the Mediterranean. It was now Henry's crucial task to ascertain what was happening.

It was not an easy assignment for Henry. Although the enemy fleet was large it still was a problematical job to locate it. Fairly quickly Henry did discover the combined fleet of over 30 ships in Cadiz harbour. He sailed *Euryalus* into the mouth of the harbour, a very risky operation in itself. His small 36 gun ship could have been sighted by the enemy, run down and captured. So Henry took great care in gleaning as much information as he could and sailed back to England. These were, of course, the days when a message had to be physically carried to its recipient and, as soon as *Euryalus* landed at Lymington, he took a carriage to London to present his findings to the Lords of the Admiralty.

As he was passing Lord Nelson's own home at Merton Park, just outside London, Henry decided to call and give him his report, even before the Lords themselves received it. It was 5 o'clock in the morning but Henry had no hesitation in rousing Nelson. The Admiral was delighted that his friend, Blackwood, had called and he was visibly excited at the prospect of carrying the fight to the French and Spanish. 'Depend on it, Blackwood, I shall yet give M. Villenueve (the French Commander) a drubbing'.[5]

Nelson, however, for all his innocent excitement, had a premonition of his own death. He had even visited his upholsters and discussed arrangements for the type of coffin he wanted when the time came. He clearly thought his time was nigh.

Before Henry returned to pick up *Euryalus*, now at Portsmouth, he visited Harriet. Navy wives were certainly tolerant and patient women – they needed to be for often they never saw their husbands from one year's end to another. Henry was a prime example and had seen very little of his wife and son. He evidently treasured the time he spent with them on that occasion.

Lord Nelson quickly set sail aboard *HMS Victory* and was met by Henry and *Euryalus* some way down the English Channel. The Admiral was anxious to bring the British fleet together at the earliest opportunity and, for the next few weeks, he pestered Blackwood to bring him as much information about the combined fleet as he could. Nelson regularly summoned Henry and his other commanders aboard *Victory* to discuss tactics in the battle which Nelson expected to happen sooner rather than later.

To move from ship to ship to attend these meetings was a very tricky operation. It all sounds very straightforward until you think what had to be done. As *Euryalus* and *Victory* and the other ships of the line sailed across the Bay of Biscay they usually found the weather unpleasant and the seas high and choppy. A captain, such as Henry, would have ordered one of his ship's small cutters to be lowered into the water. He then would have had to clamber down the rope ladder and precariously gain a footing inside the little craft. His men would then have rowed him across the stretch of sea between *Euryalus* and *Victory*. It could have been, and often was, a very uncomfortable passage, especially when he was dressed in his finery to meet around the Admiral's table. The journey could have lasted half an hour and he often would have arrived drenched to the skin, having to dry himself off before approaching the Admiral's cabin. So the oft-used phrase – 'he went aboard the Victory' – thus entailed a great deal more than meets the eye.

Once on board the Admiral's ship lengthy discussions took place nearly every day at that crucial time. When not being rowed across to *Victory*, Henry continued to closely scrutinise the enemy fleet in Cadiz. He soon discovered that there were 34 huge ships of the line and Nelson realised that the best numbers he could muster would be around 27.

As the British ships arrived in the waters off the Spanish port of Cadiz, tension rose. Nelson, never a patient man, was pacing the decks of his flagship desperate to be assured that the French and Spanish had not slipped out of Cadiz harbour. In the midst of all this frenetic activity, Nelson made Henry an offer – he wanted him to captain one of the bigger ships but, although this would have been a profitable move for Henry at any other time, he turned it down, much to Nelson's surprise. He was determined to remain with the ship and the men he knew aboard *Euryalus*. It was a sensible decision, although not without some regrets. He hoped that his refusal would not jeopardise his promotion prospects for the future. They certainly did not and his attitude brought him many plaudits, not only from his own men but also from Nelson and the Lords of the Admiralty.

The end to the watching and waiting

By 19 October 1805 the waiting game was over. Egged on by the notion that Napoleon was about to censure him for his indecision, Admiral Villeneuve ordered his fleet out of Cadiz harbour and into the Atlantic. He knew that a summons to Paris could mean the end of his naval career; it could also have meant a much worse fate for an admiral who had given sterling service to the French. The die was cast.

Henry Blackwood's report for the day was that the enemy was finally on the move. To the consternation of the British, Henry reported that not 34, but 39, ships were sailing out of Cadiz. The extra ships were smaller, but nonetheless every bit as dangerous. The scene aboard *Victory* was of an uncharacteristically calm and unruffled Nelson. He no longer pounded the upper decks. He knew the battle was about to commence and he settled himself down to await the first shots in an encounter that would be make or break for both sides. Nelson got down on his knees and prayed that Almighty God would deliver victory to the British fleet. He surveyed his fleet before him, knowing that all his masters had their orders. There could be no turning back; for Nelson there would be no turning back.

The last order he gave was to surprise his friend, Henry Blackwood. As Henry was making his crew ready aboard *Euryalus* and as he wrote yet another letter to Harriet at home, he received a command to attend his Admiral on the *Victory*. And so it was that Henry Blackwood was to spend very little time aboard his own ship during what was to be the greatest naval battle of all time. His Admiral had summoned him; his Admiral had given him an order; it was for Henry to obey. Accordingly he was taken across the heavy seas yet again by his faithful boatswain and crew to be with Nelson. Little did he know then that he was all too soon to be beside Nelson at his dying hour.

The Battle of Trafalgar

By 8 o'clock Henry was aboard *Victory* as Nelson had commanded. The Admiral was unusually apprehensive because when he set eyes on the combined fleet as it sailed out of Cadiz harbour it seemed a mightier fleet than he had imagined. But this only made him all the more determined and, having discussed the plan of campaign with his captains, including Henry, he sent them back to their own ships. All except Henry that is. He was required to be at Nelson's side.

Nelson's next act was an event which has become indelibly linked as much with the battle as with the whole story of Lord Nelson. He summoned Captain Hardy of *Victory* and Henry to his cabin and there had them witness the last codicil of his will. The words of this legal attachment to his will made interesting reading. 'I leave Emma Lady Hamilton as a legacy to my King and Country that they will give her ample provision to maintain her rank in life'.[6] Nelson's love for Emma Hamilton was the most open secret in the navy and throughout England. They had a daughter, Horatia, some years previously but she had never been given or used her father's name. In the codicil, Nelson declared that the little girl should henceforth use his surname. Hardy and Blackwood dutifully witnessed the codicil as requested by Nelson. (It transpired that these wishes of Nelson's will were never enacted and Lady Hamilton died in later years in straightened circumstances. His daughter did, however, use the Nelson name but never fully understood the part played by the Admiral in her life).

The captains, as well as the crew of the *Victory*, were extremely concerned about Nelson's safety. Henry, realising the obvious danger he was in, suggested that Nelson either go aboard *Euryalus* and use it as his flagship or, at least, not allow *Victory* to attack the enemy as the forward ship. Nelson was also wearing all his colourful sashes and medals and he was a prime target for any sharpshooter who would have easily spotted him from their vantage points at the top of the masts. In a word, he was a sitting duck.

Nelson's sense of drama never left him to the end. He directed that a special signal be sent to all his ships so he turned to his signals lieutenant and instructed him to display the message – 'England confides that every man will do his duty'. But his lieutenant told Nelson that the word 'confides' would

A battle scene at Trafalgar, 21 October 1805

need to be spelt out letter by letter on the signal flags and that the verb 'expects' would be easier and quicker to send. And so it was that the famous communication was sent – 'England expects every man will do his duty'. The requisite flags were flown and, as soon as the officers and sailors aboard all the fleet read the message, there was much spontaneous cheering and even the dancing of hornpipes and singing of sea shanties. Nelson's gift of communicating with his men remained to the end.

Thus, with the codicil signed and witnessed and the rousing communiqué sent, Nelson ordered the *Victory* into the fray. Henry watched in consternation, but not surprise, as *Victory* ploughed into the combined enemy fleet. From early in the day the battle was fierce and no quarter was given for a considerable time. Ships on both sides were severely damaged with top masts falling amongst the frightened ships' crews as they struggled to keep their guns firing.

In the midst of the smoke and mayhem, Nelson took Henry aside and uttered the immortal words – 'God bless you, Blackwood, I shall never speak to you again'.[7] Nelson then continued to stride about the *Victory's* decks encouraging his men – all the while in grave danger of being hit by an enemy sharpshooter.

Henry returned for a short time to *Euryalus*, once more rowed across the turbulent ocean by his brave seamen with the sound of battle all around. When he returned to *Victory* by early afternoon, he discovered, to his utter dismay, that Nelson had indeed been shot. A marksman from a French ship had scored a direct hit, injuring Nelson such that his spine was shot away. He had but three hours to live and, having been taken down to the already overworked surgeon and his assistants in the sickbay, he insisted that he took his place in the queue of those to be treated as was the navy custom.

He knew that his life was ebbing away and lay quietly in the arms of Captain Hardy with Henry Blackwood in close proximity. There is still some dispute whether Henry was present with Nelson at the time of his death. He certainly was not on *Victory* when the Admiral was shot but, as was fulsomely noted in a letter to Harriet, he was in attendance at the time of death – around 4.30 pm on 21 October 1805.

Admiral Collingwood now assumed command. His own ship *HMS Royal Sovereign* had already received a battering and was soon crippled. Having heard with dismay of the death of his commander, Collingwood assumed control of the battle and went aboard *Euryalus* to prosecute the fight from there. Accordingly Henry's simple frigate became the British flagship for the next ten days. *Royal Sovereign* was so badly stricken that *Euryalus* had to take it in tow although, after a week, it was able to be sufficiently repaired so as to allow it to make for England under its own power.

The battle raged all day and, in the end, the French and Spanish fleets were vanquished and the British victorious. But, without their commander at the helm, it seemed a hollow victory. Yet the British had carried the day with Killyleagh's Captain Blackwood much to the fore and always in the midst of the fray. The British ships, damaged though many of them were, managed to take a number of precious prizes in tow. These were worthwhile rewards for winning such a momentous sea fight. They looked forward to bringing them back to English ports and dividing the spoils.

But it was not to be. The notorious Bay of Biscay reared its ugly head once more. For the next four days storms and tempests roared and all the enemy ship prizes either broke their cables from the British and ran aground or simply had to be cut adrift to sink ignominiously beneath the waves. It was a truly disconsolate fleet which staggered into the southern English harbours some three weeks after the battle.

Henry had, however, another responsible job assigned to him. He was to take the *Euryalus* into Cadiz and speak to the governor to arrange a swap of prisoners. He was chosen because of his fluency in the French language which was used in Spain as the diplomatic language. He also had on board his ship the defeated enemy admirals, including Admiral Villenueve, whom Nelson had hoped to 'batter'. What with many survivors from various British ships and other enemy ships, the *Euryalus* was seriously overladen. But she returned to Falmouth five weeks after the battle much to the adulation of a grateful and adoring British public. Their mood was, of course, sombre owing to the tragic death of Lord Nelson but they did appreciate the great task that had been achieved.

The battle of Trafalgar was one of the greatest sea battles of all time. It is the best remembered sea battle and, for many, the only one they ever knew about. Lord Horatio Nelson was perhaps the best admiral that Britain ever had and everyone knows of the paintings which depict him in the arms of Captain Hardy in the bowels of that mighty ship, *Victory*. Many even recall the last words of Nelson – 'Kiss me, Hardy'. Whether or not these words were fact or fiction matters little . It was a 'must win' battle for Nelson and Britain and one which Nelson's men delivered.

In the round of decorations distributed after the dust had settled Henry was presented with a 100 guinea gold sword, an honour of which he was immensely proud. Others received baronetcies and knighthoods, but he was delighted to have been able to contribute to this wonderful triumph and to receive recognition for his efforts. What was even more pleasing, however, was his promotion, soon afterwards, to the 3rd rate 74 gun *HMS Ajax* – itself a veteran of Trafalgar.

Killyleagh's own son, Henry Blackwood, had not only been present at this magnificent battle but he had also been an integral part of the British victory that late October day two hundred years ago.

The funeral of Lord Nelson

Nelson's body had been solemnly brought back to England aboard the *Victory*. Almost three months passed, however, before the Admiral was laid to rest. The arrangements were made for a service in St. Paul's Cathedral in London on 9 January 1806. Henry was honoured by being made the trainbearer for the Commander-in-Chief of the Royal Navy, Sir Peter Parker, and his two supporters. The reason why Henry, the mere captain of frigates at Trafalgar, was asked to undertake these onerous and important duties is not recorded. It can only be surmised that it was on account of his attention to his varied responsibilities at the battle, together with his close friendship with the late Lord Nelson. He was immensely proud of this honour bestowed on him.

Henry travelled up the Thames on the barge immediately behind Nelson's body. At the lying in state he was also present and, on the day of the funeral, he sat beside Admiral Parker close to the altar in the cathedral and also witnessed the internment down in the crypt. The Cathedral was packed with people of high and lowly station representing the vast array of those whom Lord Nelson had known and loved. But there were a number of gaps in the congregation. The Royal family was not officially represented although the Prince of Wales and his brother, the Duke of Clarence, did attend in a private capacity.

Nor did the three people closest to him attend either. His estranged wife was not there because it was not then the convention for widows to be present at their husband's funeral.

Nor was his successor at Trafalgar, Admiral Lord Collingwood, in attendance for he was still at sea. And, most pointedly, neither was Lady Emma Hamilton who, of course, was not invited and who had to grieve for her lover alone. The country was pressing home its dislike, or even disgust, at this aspect of Nelson's life. They loved and adored the man as Admiral, but they shunned him because of his private morals.

The country had now said farewell to their hero of Trafalgar. Captain Henry Blackwood, too, moved on.

5.
The Tragic Loss of *HMS Ajax*

Henry was doubtless pleased to have been appointed to the 3rd rate 74 gun *Ajax*. His appointment had been announced in January 1806 but he was not aboard his new command until nine months later on the first anniversary of Trafalgar, 21 October 1806. The cause for this delay was several fold.

To begin with Henry was spending some time with his wife at their home and was finally enjoying family life again. His wife was pregnant and, in the following June, gave birth to a daughter, Henrietta. (Sadly she was to die in April 1808, aged just 22 months). His little son was now almost six years old and also destined to join the navy.

Henry had then to find well over 600 men to man his new charge and there were the usual difficulties of getting men transferred from the *Euryalus*, finding foreigners and more pressed men as sailors and dealing with a plethora of complaints and other unnecessary distractions.

By the time he was ready to take command *Ajax* was in the Mediterranean and Henry and many of his men had to sail there aboard *HMS Royal George*. After rendezvousing with Admiral Collingwood, Henry finally was mustered aboard *Ajax* on 21 October when he received his pay as a 3rd rate captain, £278 per annum, for the first time.

As was so often the case for Royal Navy captains they came in regular contact with ships which they had previously commanded. And so it was for Henry who regularly saw the *Euryalus* and even *HMS Malta*, which had formerly been the *Guillaume Tell*, captured from the French by Henry years before.

Disaster in the Dardanelles

Trouble was brewing in the eastern Mediterranean, this time with the Turks, and Collingwood had been ordered into this narrow and dangerous waterway to intimidate them. Britain was anxious to negotiate with the Turks but had so far been unsuccessful. So it was decided to take the navy there to threaten them. *Ajax* was one of the fleet which sailed into the narrows early in February 1807. What happened next was to leave an indelible mark for the rest of Henry's life and naval career.

At 9 o'clock on the evening of 14 February 1807, a fire broke out aboard *Ajax*. Before Henry and his crew could do much about it the fire had taken hold in the lower decks and was consuming the ship at an alarming speed. Henry took control of the situation giving clear signals to his men as to how best to deal with the outbreak. But, before anything could be done, the conflagration had taken a firm hold on the ship and, try as the crew might, it was not long before the vessel was engulfed. As the men – those who had not already been burned to death – retreated further and further towards the stern to avoid the flames, Henry realised that he could not save his ship. It was beginning to sink by the bow.

As the fire licked at the very feet of the crewmen huddling at the stern, so it became obvious to all that they would have to take to the water. Having searched around as much as he could to extricate as many of his men as possible, Henry himself dived into the cold waters beneath. For almost an hour he clung to a floating oar before he was rescued by a boat from *HMS Canopus,* one of many ships searching for survivors from the burning and sinking *Ajax.*

By 5 am the ship had sunk. Those who had been rescued were cared for by their fellow seamen on other ships, including Henry who was taken aboard *HMS Canopus* before being transferred to *HMS Royal George,* a huge 1st rate ship of 100 guns.

Of *Ajax's* 650 men nearly 270 were drowned or burned alive. To Henry this was a day of great sadness for he had lost many of his senior men and some of the young midshipmen whom he had been looking after and taking an interest in. Reports from the other ships' captains talked of Henry's courage in trying to save his men; of his devotion to duty; of his immense sorrow at the loss of his ship.

The subsequent enquiry exonerated Henry from all blame or negligence. The cause of the tragic loss of *HMS Ajax* had been brought about through the drunkenness of two of the ship's bakers. The fire had broken out in the bread room which was unsupervised owing to the inebriation of the men in charge. The culprits had died in the inferno.

In his letter to his wife Henry described his utter melancholy and wretchedness, his despair and grief. He was, for days, quite inconsolable but, with the help of his men and colleagues, he was soon able to overcome his distress. Nonetheless the sight of his ship ablaze in foreign waters remained with him for the rest of his life.

Back home in county Down another event occurred affecting the Blackwood family. Baroness Dorcas, Henry's mother, had died in England, aged 80, just one week before the *Ajax* was lost. Henry did not, of course, learn of his mother's passing for many weeks and, in fact, had instructed his wife to inform all the Ballyleidy and Killyleagh family members about the fire which had occurred on his ship and the circumstances surrounding it. Once more we can see how slow and cumbersome communications were in the early years of the nineteenth century. In fact it was probably up to six months before Henry received the sad news. He had seen so little of his mother throughout his entire life – such was the lot of the naval captain.

Henry completed his tour of duty aboard a number of other ships and performed an excellent service to them and their captains. The Turks, soon after the disastrous loss of the *Ajax*, came out to fight the British fleet but were soundly defeated. It was time for Henry to return home arriving at Penzance at the end of April aboard the little brig, *L'Espoir*, bringing despatches for the Admiralty from Admiral Collingwood which announced the news of their victory in the Dardanelles.

Hardly had he returned home to Surrey to see his family than he was back in London having himself weighed once more. These visits were becoming part of a ritual every time he set foot on English soil. One might even say that it showed a certain eccentricity in the man from county Down.

But much more importantly and seriously Henry got to work looking out for the welfare of his survivors from the *Ajax* and also, of course, for the families of those who had died. He wrote reams to the Lords at the Admiralty and, by his sheer persistence, he was able to alleviate the difficulties experienced by many a young widow or an elderly parent. Had it not been for his persuasive powers, many relatives would only have received very minimal support from the Navy Board.

He championed another crusade. Improved safety conditions were paramount, in Henry's eyes, in order to obviate the tragedy which had been visited upon the *Ajax*. He did not just talk about his views for improvements; he drew up plans for them and sent them to the Sea Lords. For example he suggested that, instead of so many solid walls beneath decks, there should be more of the partitions made of latticework thus ensuring that any fire or emergency could be discovered more quickly. Their Lordships were impressed by Henry's proposals and saw to it that they were implemented. As it happened a new 3rd rate ship of the line was being completed, *HMS Warspite*, and the improvements recommended by Henry were put into practice. This very costly new ship (at £60,000, a great sum in those days) also needed a captain and, to Henry's obvious delight, he was himself appointed to the post. *Warspite* was to be his 18th ship – he was now 38 years old and a veteran of 28 years in His Majesty's Navy.

Births and a death – and a return to the Mediterranean

One of the adaptations added to the *Warspite* (and to other ships of the line) was the change in colour of the gun carriages. This may not seem a very innovative change from black to yellow but many lives were saved because of this improvement to a ship's design. In battle, or even when walking on deck in the dark, sailors and officers frequently tripped on the carriage rails because of the difficulty in seeing them. Simply by painting the rails either yellow or some other light colour made the rails much easier to see and injuries were consequently avoided.

As he manned his new ship replete this time with a ship's band and taking on board a number of the sons of his friends and acquaintances as midshipmen, Henry heard that he had been appointed Naval Officer and Harbour Master of the West Indian islands of St. Thomas and St. John. He was never in his life to visit these faraway islands but he received, nonetheless, the financial benefits of his position. This was a prime example of a sinecure – really receiving money for doing nothing, a not unusual perk for senior officers in the Navy. He had previously unsuccessfully applied for the post of Governor of Dominica, also in the Caribbean.

He was able to spend some time at home during 1808 and it was in that year that joy and sadness intervened yet again. In April his second son, Arthur, was born at almost exactly the same time as little Henrietta, not yet two, died. Sudden deaths were a common occurrence in every social class in those days. There is no record of the cause of his daughter's death but it was, most probably, some childhood illness which today would be simply treated. Nor is there any record of Henry's visiting county Down in that year – it seems unlikely. Spending precious time with his wife and family would have taken preference over travelling to Ireland.

Warspite eventually got under way patrolling the English Channel and home waters or undertaking boring escort duties. But at least it meant that he did have more time ashore. His family was further added to in May 1809 when another baby son, Francis, was born. Harriet was now over 40 years old but seemed to be enjoying motherhood although she would have had staff to assist her.

Once more service in the Mediterranean beckoned; once more it meant a very long time away from home. It would be over two years until he would return to British shores. His commander-in-chief, Lord Collingwood, died at this time, something which saddened Henry. The two men had got on well together and Collingwood had much to be thankful to Henry for after the battle of Trafalgar.

In the Mediterranean *Warspite* was, at last, able to take a number of prizes. This expanse of sea was full of unfriendly craft and many fell foul of *Warspite*. In a short period of two weeks in March 1813 (on a second tour of the Mediterranean) *Warspite* took five prizes and the money which accrued from these various captures helped to swell Henry's funds as well as those of his men. It was a lucrative area to be assigned to – and Henry knew it.

There were, of course, darker and more dangerous moments. The French port of Toulon was always full of enemy, or potential enemy, ships and, from time to time, they set out from harbour with a view to harassing the British ships. On one such occasion a large number of French ships did appear only to turn tail and run back to port to avoid the British ships. There was a long running dispute over this particular episode and doubt was cast, wrongly it eventually transpired, on Henry's handling of the fight and the actual number of French ships involved. The inference was that Henry had botched an encounter against a small group of French ships. But he was vindicated after a lengthy legal process.

Henry persisted in complaining to the Lords of the Admiralty at the way he was being treated and at the mundane work he and *Warspite* had often to undertake. His petulance could easily have jeopardised his entire naval career had it not been for his out and out decency and fairness and also for his new found friendship with Henry Addington, the Prime Minister. Henry also cultivated friendships with the Prince of Wales and his brother, the Duke of Clarence, later to become King William IV. He had even taken on an illegitimate son of the Duke's as a midshipman aboard *Warspite.*

The general tenor of life in the King's Navy was, in some ways, deteriorating. Henry continued to do his duty to the best of his ability and follow orders scrupulously. Yet there was unpleasantness and back biting. Perhaps the fact that he was a kindly man was going against him. The Duke of Clarence's mistress, the mother of the young midshipman attached to Henry's ship, even had the effrontery to describe Captain Blackwood as a tyrant who regularly flogged his middies. Nothing could have been further from the truth and the Duke was obviously satisfied enough to send his son to Henry. In the event, the boy blossomed under Henry's guiding hand after the initial fright of joining the navy. Sadly the boy died at the early age of 20 a few years later of natural causes.

After over five years on *Warspite* Henry at length resigned as captain of the ship in November 1813. He had never taken such a drastic step before but he felt sufficiently secure, not to mention fed up, to take this resolute action.

Ostensibly he had resigned because he had urgent business back in Ireland. He had been pursuing the Lords of the Admiralty to give him enough leave to deal with his Irish responsibilities. Having baulked him request after request, Henry took the matter into his own hands and quit the service.

All we know is that his business in Ireland, probably Dublin, required a court appearance, but what exactly the case was is unknown. And whether he visited Ballyleidy and Killyleagh is not known either. It could have been that he did but, in truth, such a long journey up north would probably not have been undertaken. At best letters would have been sent to inform the family of his whereabouts and of his progress in his naval career.

In March of 1813, there was a further addition to his own family – the birth of his daughter, Harriet, who was to be his last child. He was delighted and at least found time to savour the joys of parenthood.

Rear Admiral Henry Blackwood

Having resigned from the service Henry must have thought that he had burned his boats and that he would no longer be persona grata with the Navy Board. But his persistence and thorough determination had worked in his favour, much to his surprise. At the age of 44 the Honourable Henry Blackwood was not only in favour but found himself in a most important and key posting. It seems that his cultivation of friendships with the great and the good had paid off. In April 1814 the Lords of the Admiralty appointed Henry's new friend, the Duke of Clarence, to the position of Channel Fleet Admiral. And the Duke refused to go to sea without Henry as his Captain of the Fleet, a posting which the new Admiral was entitled to make. The Lords had no option but to agree and Captain Blackwood was appointed to the position.

The first job Henry undertook was to arrange the state visit of Tsar Alexander of Russia and King Frederick of Prussia. The European powers had at last brought Napoleon Bonaparte to his knees and would soon exile the French dictator to Elba. Thus it was an opportune time for such a visit to the Court of St James; and also an opportunity for Henry Blackwood to excel. The idea of making all the preparations for such a prestigious event appealed to Henry and he did not let his monarch and the Duke of Clarence down.

In the early 1800s state visits were as important as nowadays. But the state of travel in those days was a far cry from being whisked away from Russia to London in a large jet aircraft. The Tsar and the Prussian king had been in Paris to sign the treaty which forced Napoleon into exile and so it was from there that the royal entourages made their tortuous way to the channel port of Boulogne and thence to the English capital.

All details for the welcoming of the foreign visitors were made by Henry. There were welcoming parties, naval reviews and state banquets to be arranged. There were orders to be given as to what dress to wear on which particular occasion. There were festivities to be put in train. It seems that the Tsar was a poor traveller and an even worse sailor. He was seasick and then so exhausted that he had to miss out on some of the celebrations. For days the country feted the royal guests and, in the end, after all the food, wine and frivolity, it was agreed by everyone, even the haughty Lords of the Admiralty, that Captain Blackwood's arrangements had been first class. The visit had been a resounding success and, as a reward, Henry was promoted to Rear Admiral. When the dust had settled and the royal personages safely returned to mainland Europe, Rear Admiral of the Blue Henry Blackwood had time to reflect on his good fortune.

He was now an admiral, the lowest ranking one to be sure, but an admiral all the same. A 'Blue' admiral was entitled to fly his own pennant on the rearmost mast of a ship and then, as he progressed to the 'White' and eventually to the 'Red', his pennant moved too – at length to fly from the foremast. His friends and former crewmen, when they heard the news, were delighted to hear of Henry's well deserved advancement.

His duties to attend to kings, princes and tsars continued throughout the month of June 1814. The Prince Regent, later King George IV, and the Duke of Clarence, as well as entertaining the Russian and Prussian heads of state, also had to ensure the safe return of the exiled King Louis XVIII of France and his huge entourage from England to his own capital in Paris. Henry consummately carried out these tasks with ease and aplomb. He received his next reward early in July once all the hubbub was over.

Along with four other of his colleagues, Henry was granted 'the dignity of becoming a Baronet of the United Kingdom of Great Britain and Ireland'. He was indeed proud of his achievement as a seventh son of a baronet had little likelihood of ever succeeding to his father's title. The Honourable Henry Blackwood had gained nobility in his own right.

A holiday in Ireland

Following the departure of the royal visitors, Henry applied for leave which was granted. It was infinitely easier to be granted time off when he was on shore in England. There being no other pressing business with the Duke of Clarence, Henry retired to his home in Esher in Surrey. He settled down to domestic bliss with his wife and children. He even decided to spend a great deal of money in buying a magnificent carriage festooned, naturally enough, with his new noble insignia.

Whilst at home he continued to fight the causes of his seamen. Throughout his life many of his men wrote to him with their own distressing stories. Henry never failed to take an interest in their plight and during this extended leave he was involved in lots of worthy cases. For example he could never see why the navy should be reduced in numbers so drastically in time of peace compared with the army. When the navy was scaled down it meant that thousands of sailors, who had fought for King and country, were rendered unemployed. There was no effective severance pay or even a decent pension. They were often left penniless with little or no prospect of work. Whether Henry was successful in his endeavours is a moot point. The Lords of the Admiralty never possessed that quality of mercy and justice which Henry so espoused. Suffice it to say that whenever he did champion a cause he made a certain amount of progress. He was not a person to be defeated by bureaucracy.

The Blackwoods then, towards the end of 1814, set out for what must have been the only family holiday they ever had to his homes in county Down. Lady Harriet accompanied her husband but it is uncertain whether or not any of his children came. However, on balance, it does seem possible that his youngest children may well have come, although little Harriet was still an infant. The journey would have been a trial across the roads of England by coach and four and then on a ferry ship over to Ireland, possibly Belfast. His eldest brother, Lord Dufferin, would have seen to it that the family carriages were at the docks to bring his brother's family down to Ballyleidy.

The Ballyleidy House where Henry spent much of his childhood had been destroyed by fire in the last years of the 18th century and had been replaced by a much bigger and grander mansion. In the years after Henry's death and in the lifetime of his great nephew, Lord Frederick Blackwood, 1st Marquess of Dufferin and Ava (1826-1902) the house was renamed Clandeboye House and so it remains to this day.

Whilst on holiday in county Down there is always the speculation that he and his wife visited their relatives in Killyleagh Castle. It seems unthinkable that a visit was not made and that a few days would have been spent in the village where Henry had spent so many happy times in his early years. Henry also talked politics for his brother, James, Lord Dufferin, was an MP at the time. He even took up correspondence with his great friend, Henry Addington, by now Lord Sidmouth, who was still a member of the government.

When the Christmas festivities were at an end, Henry and his family left to go to Dublin. Again this would have been a journey of some days over the rough roads of counties Down, Louth, Meath and Dublin. When there they stayed in accommodation in Harcourt Street and Henry made sure to be introduced to those of importance in the Irish capital, including the Lord Lieutenant. He continued to have an eye for those splendid occasions and the chance to wear his finery and newly acquired insignia of nobility.

By March, however, they had all returned to Esher after lots more time spent in draughty carriages and uncomfortable ferries.

By now Henry had been ashore for by far the longest time in his career. In June 1815, Napoleon Bonaparte, who had escaped from Elba and raised an army back in France, continued to be the scourge of Europe. But he was soundly defeated at the battle of Waterloo on 18 June 1815 and once more exiled, for the last time, to the wastes of the island of St. Helena in the South Atlantic.

Henry applied for a further extension of leave and, when it was granted without so much as a squeak from the Lords, he set off for a stay in France. There he remained for almost a year and absolutely nothing is known of what he did whilst there. This is another tantalising episode in Henry Blackwood's life. We know so much from all his diaries and logs from his various naval commands and yet, when it comes to his private life, we are often in the realms of nothing more than rumour and conjecture. We do know that he was most proficient in the French language and it could well be that he felt the need to take time out and perhaps look up former friends and acquaintances who lived in that country – and to brush up on his French. It is fairly certain that Lady Harriet did not accompany her husband on his continental sojourn from which he returned in February 1817.

Henry had not been at sea for over three years by now and this situation was still not about to change. At home again, although he may have gone back to France for a month or two during the summer months of 1817, Henry continued to correspond with the Lords of the Admiralty concerning the fortunes – or misfortunes – of many of his former sailors. He appealed on their behalf on all sorts of causes and his hard work was appreciated by his men.

Henry Martin Blackwood, Henry's first son, was now himself in the navy. His father's influence had obviously carried the day and he was able to rely on his renowned parent to pull a few strings. By 1817, when the boy was 16 years old, Henry made arrangements for his son to be sent to *HMS Ganymede* which was, in his estimation, a suitable posting presumably with a kindly and caring captain. Young Henry was to make a name for himself as his father had done.

Further Royal appointments

In 1818, Sir Henry was made a Groom of the Chamber by the Prince Regent. These quaint sounding positions in the Royal Household brought prestige to the appointee as well as extra income. For Henry both points pleased him. For the remainder of his life he held this appointment during the last years of King George III's reign and those of King George IV and King William IV. His extra salary was £500 per annum which was a considerable sum in those days. As Groom, Henry was required to spend regular periods of two weeks at the royal palaces attending to the whims of his monarch and dining with the members of the Royal Family. Henry revelled in his new found position – it appealed to his sense of importance and to his unbridled vanity.

In 1819 he had yet more cause for celebration. He was promoted to Rear Admiral of the White – his pennant would now move forward one mast – and he was no longer on the bottom rung of the admiral's ladder. And to crown this outstanding year, the Prince Regent (who was, of course, the acting monarch, or regent, owing to King George III's enduring illnesses) 'was pleased to invest Rear-Admiral the Honourable Sir Henry Blackwood, Bart. with the ensigns of a knight commander of the Most Honourable Military Order of the Bath'.[8]

His investiture was an affair full of the grandest pomp and ceremony and his family was rightly proud of their honoured kinsman, Sir Henry Blackwood, KCB.

6.
A Voyage to India

Henry had now been at home or at least not in command of a ship for the longest time in his life. It had been six years since he resigned from *HMS Warspite* and been promoted to Rear Admiral. In the intervening years he had risen through the ranks, been decorated by the acting monarch and had, most fortuitously, been present to see his youngest children grow up.

He was, by the end of 1819, almost 50 years of age and clearly wondered if he would ever be given another naval appointment. He was probably tempted to stay at home for he had lots of money and sinecures to look after his family, but there was also a part of him that longed to be back aboard ship and on the high seas serving his King and country.

Then he did receive the call to return to service. During the latter half of 1818 came the announcement that he had been appointed Commander-in-Chief, India. This was a prestigious and a very senior posting. He accepted although he had doubts about leaving home after spending the past six years at home with his family. Many arrangements had to be made which took an interminable time. He had, after all, to move halfway round the world to the outmost reaches of the Empire. And he had to make the hardest decision of his life – whether or not to take Lady Harriet with him.

Henry was doubtless chosen for this far-off posting because of his ability to use his initiative and his total loyalty to the Crown. He had proved himself over the years in many stations. He was a true leader of men and one who was respected and liked by those under his command. The Commander-in-Chief India had to make decisions on his own. He could not wait for letters to be sent to and from India. It often took six months just for a letter just to reach England from the sub continent. There was no time to waste on many an occasion and, in effect, the holder stood in loco regis (acting for the King). Sir Henry Blackwood could be trusted and was the perfect man for the job.

He accepted the posting with all its advantages and all its disadvantages and stepped aboard *HMS Leander* on 30 December 1819 to be taken out to his new command in the Far East.

How the Rear Admiral nearly never made it to India

HMS Leander was a fine, and fairly newly built, 4th rate frigate under the command of Captain Charles Richardson who was well acquainted with his ship. Henry took with him a small entourage including his nephew, Price, the son of his brother Hans. Young Price was appointed Flag Officer and was delighted to be aboard ship with his illustrious uncle. The *Leander* finally got under way from Spithead on 6 January 1820. (January 1820 was a traumatic month for the United Kingdom. The old King George, having reigned for 60 years died to be succeeded by his son, the Prince Regent, who had ruled in his father's stead since 1811. The new King became George IV).

Henry then had the small matter of saying goodbye to his wife and children. We can only imagine what an emotional moment it was even for such a hardened sailor as himself. The farewells thus made, the adventure began.

The prospect of a very long and tedious journey to the Far East was certainly enlivened by an incident off the island of Madeira, only a few days out of their English port. In retrospect Henry Blackwood was to experience the very worst occurrence of his entire naval career – and that included the dreadful and horrific fire and sinking of *HMS Ajax* in 1807. It was to be the most heart-stopping moment of all.

The *Leander* was unfortunate enough to get into some difficulty as it approached Funchal, the capital of Madeira. A series of mishaps over hawsers and anchors suddenly propelled the ship towards the rocks. There remained insufficient sail to properly steer the ship and, had it not been for Henry and Captain Richardson making a very precise decision in a split second, then the vessel would have been crushed against the rocks. Henry's words immediately after the near miss – 'a biscuit could have been thrown on board from the cliffs'[9] – graphically describes the dilemma they were in. Suitably chastened and relieved the ship cleared the island and headed for the remainder of an otherwise unremarkable voyage.

One of the vagaries of serving in the Royal Navy was the fact that the new Commander-in-Chief was not entitled to his pay in that rank until he had actually reached the relevant longitude. As he sailed out Henry was, in effect, still a Vice Admiral but, at the beginning of April, the *Leander* passed the position 60 degrees east. Henry was at last the Commander-in-Chief and could now fly his appropriate pennant and draw his appropriate pay.

His first port of call, and the one where he was to remain for most of his time in the Indian sub continent, was Trincomalee, not in India itself but on the island of Ceylon (Sri Lanka today). The first shock was the wretchedness of his accommodation. He could not understand how his predecessor could possibly have lived in such a dilapidated place. His correspondence began. Although his position warranted urgent action he felt, nonetheless, that his complaints should be addressed to the Lords Commissioners back in London.

His was to be a miserable tour of duty. He had nearly lost his life early on the journey; he had to live in what he considered to be little better than a hovel; he now started to suffer from the ravages of the heat and sweaty conditions of that part of the world. He felt ill; he did not relish the prospect of tiger hunts; he had premonitions of his wife's ill health back at home. Henry Blackwood knew he had made the wrong decision in accepting this distant posting. He wanted to be back at home. But he had to put on a brave face for he had his duties to perform.

He had to continue to take care of those around him. His men succumbed to various diseases; many died and many others were adversely affected for the rest of their lives. Cholera, for example, was endemic. It seemed that half the population suffered either from its ravages or from some other incurable malady.

He carried out his responsibilities throughout the region travelling aboard the *Leander*. He visited the islands of the Indian Ocean, the huge landmass of India and the jungles of Burma, always returning to his house in Ceylon. The Commander-in-Chief could not be faulted for his attention to his tasks and, even when he accompanied hundreds of men and servants on those interminable game hunts when scores of wild animals were needlessly slaughtered, he acquiesced in fulfilling everything that was expected of a man of his rank and position. Many a time he yearned for home and for the green hills of county Down and Ballyleidy House and the shores of Strangford Lough and the comforts of Killyleagh castle.

Probably for the first time in his life, Henry became paranoid. When letters did eventually arrive from his wife, he discovered that she was unwell. The health of his children was also giving rise for concern. In his bachelor accommodation in Ceylon he, too, felt poorly. Now he morbidly thought that he might die in the Indian subcontinent and desperately tried to settle his will. Whether or not Lady Harriet and the children were actually as ill as he made out, Henry nonetheless still felt uneasy. He wanted to return home.

When writing to the Lords Commissioners he indicated, in a forceful manner, that he had no desire to stay in Ceylon and he wished most fervently to be recalled. The letters, of course, took many months to reach the British Isles and, when he received their reply, he was relieved to know that his recall was imminent. He wrote continually to his old friend, Lord Sidmouth, on all manner of subjects but chiefly beseeching him to keep an eye on his family back home. Henry Sidmouth must have been a very patient and valued friend to be able to tolerate the frequent and lengthy missives from Ceylon from Henry Blackwood.

As we look back almost 200 years to this period in history we will find it impossible to understand the mood of men like Henry in such a far flung part of the world. This was real isolation with few mitigating circumstances. His very house was uncomfortable and his friends out there few and far between.

His purgatory came to an end when, on 10 August 1822, he set off aboard *Leander* for Europe and England. He arrived back on 13 December 1822 in time to spend Christmas with Harriet and the children. Fortunately there were no scares like the near disaster off Madeira on the outward journey. The sea voyage was as tedious as ever and Henry would have spent the time entertaining himself and his fellow officers on the ship.

It must have been a considerable relief for Henry when he saw the English coast come into view after more than 4 months on the high seas. The harbour at Portsmouth must have seemed like paradise to him. He could not wait to join the Christmas festivities with his wife and family whom he had not seen for nearly three years.

Back home in England

Henry's tour of duty in the Far East was relatively short compared to the service of other Commanders-in-Chief. But he felt he had done his duty and so he had. He had done his best to improve the lot of the inhabitants of that region and to serve and represent his monarch there. Back home he sensed that his days at sea were over and he was determined to enjoy his family for as long as he could. His son Francis, now aged 13, had joined the navy and his father did everything he could to ensure the best possible chances for him. He, too, was to go on to do well in the service as the older Henry Martin had done.

There were very few duties required of Henry after his return. He did not complain – he wanted to enjoy his new found freedom at home with his family and friends. In May 1824 the Duke of Clarence summoned him to Plymouth where His Royal Highness was being shown the *Comet* which was the navy's first steam vessel. As senior officer, Henry accompanied his royal master on a short voyage on this new fangled ship – a sign of things to come. This was a crossroads for ships of the Royal Navy as wooden vessels would, in a few years, become part of naval history. Steam and iron would soon rule the waves. Henry waves. Henry had lived to see this significant change in the running of a world class navy.

In May 1825, when Henry was in his 55th year he was promoted to Vice Admiral of the Blue. He had reached yet another rung in the ladder and was rightly proud of all his achievements. He now earned almost £600 per annum as an admiral. It seemed an age since he joined the service as a very young and innocent midshipman nearly 45 years earlier.

That same year the Blackwoods took a house in a fashionable part of London at 7 Cornwall Terrace which was to remain the family home for the rest of their lives. In the intervening years Henry and his family had regularly visited other members of the family, mostly those in England. In the years since his return from the Far East, it seems unlikely that he went over to Ireland. His only contacts were by letter with his brothers in county Down, in Ballyleidy and Killyleagh.

Henry followed the progress of many of his young relatives who were in the navy. He was able to vouch for them and ensure promotions for them, although he never put his kinsmen's claims before those of any other deserving young men. Sir Henry Blackwood was a real favourite both as an influential uncle and as a caring former captain to hundreds of sailors. To count Henry as their friend and confidant was an honour they cherished.

He was a popular captain and a true friend. Even the Lords of the Admiralty in their lofty towers in London had to concede that there was no more worthy advocate for the men of the service, regardless of rank. They had received hundreds, if not thousands, of letters from Captain Blackwood over many years. Many had exasperated them; many had affronted and challenged them; many had even made them angry. But, in the end, they knew that his persistence had paid off and the conditions for sailors, of every rank and station, had been improved by that hardworking, tenacious and resolute gentleman, Sir Henry Blackwood.

7.
A Final Promotion and his last Journey to Ireland

Henry had spent over four years at home since his Far Eastern command. Perhaps, he considered, there were would be no more appointments for him in the navy. But in 1827 word came that one of the four so-called Home Commands was vacant and that he was to be promoted to the post at the Nore. He felt honoured that he had been chosen for this posting and looked forward to it. He moved to Admiralty House in Rochester and answered muster aboard his flagship docked there, *HMS Prince Regent*.

The role of Commander-in-Chief of the Nore meant that Henry had responsibility for all naval establishments along the North Sea coast of England as well as the massive dockyard at Chatham. It was not a very exciting position but it was an important one. He immediately set about improving his house at Rochester and then started to think about the job in hand.

Henry had, throughout his entire life, been anxious that His Majesty's ships were safe vessels for their crews. He had been pleased to see that many of his suggestions had been implemented and that safety had become the watchword of the navy.

As Commander-in-Chief of the Nore he now had added clout to make yet more improvements. He wasted no time in discussing with his senior men what needed to be done. He listened, as always, to what the sailors themselves had to say. He thought that those ideas from the men who had to sail the ships were usually more relevant and necessary than those made by the desk-bound chiefs at the Admiralty.

One cause for concern for sailors when they were firing the cannons was the difficulty in getting the guns to fire at the correct trajectory. In other words, they wanted the weapons to fire in the direction they were pointed rather than firing too high or too low. The experts were brought in to make sure that the guns in future did fire where they were pointed and this not only improved their aim but it also saved countless gunners from needless death and injury. This was but one of the improvements aboard ship which enhanced the lot of the crewmen. Henry's chief concern was not with what the ships looked like aesthetically but how safely they performed whilst ensuring the safety of the crew.

Henry was still attached to the King's staff and often was in attendance at social events. There were many visits by members of foreign royalty and there were very few European monarchs whom Henry had not met. These affairs were sumptuous and lavish and Henry was in his element. He loved dressing up in all his regalia and mixing with the most important personages in the country at some splendid soiree or other.

In June 1830 King George IV died and he was succeeded by Henry's friend the Duke of Clarence who had ascended the throne as King William IV. Henry remained a Groom for the new king and continued to undertake his regular duties at the royal palaces when his turn came round. He and his wife were still at Rochester, although they stayed from time to time in their London home.

Something which greatly pleased Henry was the appointment of his new secretary – his son Henry Martin. The young man was now 30 years old with a wife and family of his own but it was a measure of his father's confidence in him when he came to join his household. This meant, too, that the young Henry could spend time with his own family rather than be sailing all over the world and rarely having the opportunity to see his wife and children. It was a shrewd move on Sir Henry's part.

In the summer of 1830, shortly after the coronation of the new king, Henry received his final promotion to Vice Admiral of the White. He then resigned his post at the Nore after three years in charge. He was now fully retired. There would be no more calls to serve the navy which he had served since 1781, a period just short of 50 years. It had been a remarkable career and he could look back with pride on these years of faithful service.

In January 1832 Henry was, once more, decorated by the king who made him a KGCH — a Knight Grand Cross of the Royal Hanoverian Guelphic Order. And with the Order, the highest of the four classes, came yet more impressive regalia. Henry could now wear the wide blue silk sash and eight pointed star with its handsome gold and blue enamelled cross.

Death in the rolling hills of Down

The last recorded letters written by Henry Blackwood concerned the needs of old comrades. It was what Henry did best. Looking after the needs of his men and those without whom the navy could never have functioned, seemed to be his role in life.

In November 1832, Henry's son, Henry Martin, contracted typhoid (some say typhus) fever. The disease, probably in his system from his service abroad, became highly contagious. It was considered wise for the young man to go away from his family to recover lest they became infected. He spoke to his father for advice and, without hesitation, Sir Henry contacted his own family back in county Down. It seemed that there were no children then in residence at Ballyleidy and it was decided that he should bring his son across the Irish Sea to recover in the peace and tranquillity of the rolling hills of Down.

They arrived at the beginning of December and Henry set about the task of nursing his son back to health. As his son improved, however, the disease struck Sir Henry himself and he succumbed on 13 December 1832, just a few days before his 62nd birthday. It seemed a cruel twist of fate that the caring father, keen to ensure his son's return to health, should himself be afflicted and pay the ultimate price. The family at Ballyleidy was devastated and, when the news arrived with Lady Harriet in London, she was heartbroken. Her loving, caring husband, the friend of the highest and the lowest in the land, had so suddenly been called away.

The funeral at the parish church in Killyleagh

Like so much of Sir Henry Blackwood's life there are gaps in the chronicles of his private life. The funeral service took place within three or four days of his death. Consequently there would not have been time for his wife and his English relatives to travel to Ireland for the service. Only members of his Irish family were in attendance.

Henry Blackwood's remains were transported from Ballyleidy along the narrow roads of mid Down to the fishing village where he had been born. Killyleagh was in mourning. One of its famous sons was returning for the last time. As the cortege reached the top of Church Hill, the crowds pushed forwards to catch a last glimpse of their own son who had served with distinction with Nelson at Trafalgar and who had given stalwart service to King and country.

The parish church of St John the Evangelist in Killyleagh stands in a commanding position overlooking the harbour and the wide stretches of lovely Strangford Lough. Originally built in 1640 and only recently substantially rebuilt just a few years before, this imposing cruciform church was the place of worship for the members of the established Church of Ireland congregation. The rector then was the Reverend Edward Hincks, the famous Egyptologist, who officiated.

Following the service, Sir Henry Blackwood was laid to rest in the family vault in the parish graveyard within sight of the castle where was born. As they dispersed the people looked back for one last time to remember a man of great worth who was loved by all. He would be sorely missed. The loneliest and most poignant figure of all was his son, Henry Martin, who remained and wept over the grave of his father who had sacrificed his all to come to his own son's aid. He knew, however, that his father would have counted it but loss not to have rendered this paternal service – even although it had taken his own life.

Henry Blackwood, sailor and friend, had departed this mortal life. What remained was a legacy of service and devotion, not only to those whom he loved, but also to the thousands of ordinary sailors he had helped and befriended over his half century in the navy. It was an inheritance few would ever emulate.

The memorials

A fine memorial was erected by his family in the parish church not long after his death. It stands in the church today as one of four Blackwood magnificent marble plaques adorning the east wall of the south transept. The wording satisfactorily sums up the character of this fine man.

> *To the memory of Vice Admiral the Honble. Sir Henry Blackwood, Bart. whose remains are deposited in the family vault adjoining this church. He was born at Killyleagh in the year 1767, the seventh son of Sir John Blackwood, Bart. and Dorcas, Baroness DUFFERIN AND CLANEBOYE. At the age of eleven years he entered the naval service and became in after life one of its most distinguished commanders. Valiant, generous and warm-hearted, prompt and decided in danger, but never rash, he obtained respect as well as confidence of those with whom he served, he rejoiced to encourage merit and promote the interests of the deserving. Beloved by his family, admired by all, his memory will long be cherished in the domestic circle; and in the annals of Britain's naval glory his name will stand recorded with the foremost of her heroes. He died at Ballyleidy, of typhus fever on the 13th of December 1832. He was a Knight Commander of the Order of the Bath, and a Knight Grand Cross of the Royal Hanoverian Guelphic Order.*

There are a number of other Blackwood family memorials in the parish church which were added in the years following Sir Henry's death. His nephew, Robert Temple Blackwood, a son of his brother, Hans, was killed at the battle of Waterloo on 18 June 1815, aged just 23. The graphic description of his final moments are written in a little Ulster Architectural Heritage Society book – 'Clandeboye'. 'The eldest son Robert was carried off by a French cannon ball at Waterloo'.[10]

Another nephew, Hans, a soldier, died of fever in Naples in 1820 when he was just 27.

Henry's second eldest brother, James Stevenson Blackwood, Baron Dufferin is also commemorated in the church. He died, after Henry, in 1836, aged 81. Hans, whose two sons are remembered above, died in Dublin in 1839 aged 81 and another memorial was raised to him.

Price Blackwood, another nephew of Henry's, is also recalled on a memorial. He died, aged 47, in 1841. He had been in the navy and had risen to the rank of captain. He was the 4th Baron Dufferin. It was Price who had married the Irish playwright, Richard B. Sheridan's granddaughter, Helen.

There is also an inscription below the window in the north side of the nave to the 6th Baron, Frederick Hamilton Temple Blackwood (1826-1902) who was made the first Marquis of Dufferin and Ava and who was Henry's great nephew. He had a glittering career as Governor General of Canada, ambassador to Russia and Constantinople and Viceroy of India. It was he who changed the name of the family home from Ballyleidy to Clandeboye and who sold off most of the family's 18,000 acres of land.

All these illustrious men – there are no memorials to the great women of the family, not even the first Baroness, Dorcas, Henry's mother – have a permanent place in the church in Killyleagh. Their memorials are magnificent and worthy and remind the people of Killyleagh of the powerful and famous sons who lived and died in their own little village overlooking Strangford Lough.

In later years a further grand memorial was raised in no less a place as Westminster Abbey in London to Admiral Nelson's only Irish captain, the Honourable Sir Henry Blackwood. Lady Blackwood had caused the commemorative plaque to be placed with the full consent of the cathedral authorities and, above all, of the grateful citizens of the capital.

They, too, like the people of Killyleagh, can also stand and stare at the comforting words reminding them of the brave and good Sir Henry Blackwood.

The family legacy

Lady Blackwood continued to live at their London home until her death, aged 84, in 1851. She had outlived her husband by almost 20 years. Henry's son, Henry Martin, had distinguished himself in His Majesty's navy and had risen to the rank of Post Captain by the year 1827. Sadly he died, aged just 49 just after his stepmother, the woman who had raised him, in 1851. He oft remembered the life of his dear father who had given his own life that his son would live.

Henry's other sons, Arthur and Francis, made names for themselves too. Arthur joined the Civil Service and had a brilliant career there and Francis entered the navy like his father and rose to the rank of Post Captain himself.

The generations of Blackwoods continue to this day.

The Henry Blackwood memorial in Killyleagh Parish Church

Dr Henry Cooke

1.
An Exceptional Man

People in Killyleagh often mention the name Cooke when they speak of 1st Killyleagh's fine church hall in Plantation Street. Those who attend the church, or who visit it, see the words 'Cooke Memorial Hall' emblazoned in bold letters just inside the hall doors. When the minister, in his weekly announcements, gives details of the next week's events, many are scheduled to take place in the Cooke Hall.

But do the members of the congregation really know who Cooke was. For that matter do the people of Killyleagh ever think about this man Cooke. In all probability very few know much about him. The members of church session and others in the congregation with a historical bent will know something of the man – he was a minister of the church; he played a significant role in Ireland's 19th century Presbyterianism; he left his name prominently upon the church premises. These reminiscences are accurate enough but there is more to Cooke than a name inside a door.

Henry Cooke's legacy to the Presbyterian Church in Ireland is outstanding. In truth, had it not been for Henry Cooke, the future for the Presbyterians in Ireland would have been radically different. Their strong position in the life of Christians in Ireland, and in Northern Ireland in particular, owes almost everything to the determination and tenacity of this extraordinary man.

Henry Cooke was not born in Killyleagh; he was not even born in county Down. He was born, the youngest of John and Jane Cooke's two sons and two daughters, on 11 May 1788 near Maghera in county Londonderry. His father, who also had one son from his first marriage after his first wife had died young, was a plain man and a sturdy farmer. His mother, however, was a powerful and ambitious woman who soon realised the true potential of her youngest child. It was she who taught Henry the rudiments of Ireland's history.

Henry proved to be an intelligent and clever child and was very keen to learn. He was a born leader – even in those early days. After a short time spent in the local infant school he was enrolled at the grandly described 'classical seminary' in Tobermore, five long and weary miles from home. The school building itself, however, was anything but grand. It was nothing more than a rough and basic thatched house with no windows and large, hard stones for seats. His teacher, a Roman Catholic man, was a most enthusiastic and scholarly man who soon had Henry learning Virgil and Homer by heart. Henry's education was in very capable hands.

The daily journey to school was formidable. Not only had he to walk, run or even go on stilts the ten miles return each day to and from school, but he had to make the trek in all weathers. There was often wind, rain and snow to impede his progress and, halfway to the school, he had to cross the Moyola river which was frequently in spate. On one occasion he almost drowned when he fell into the river's raging torrent. Life was indeed hardy for many children in the days of the late 18th century in rural Ireland.

During his schooldays Henry experienced many of the dangers and rigours of the chaos and mayhem then existing in Ireland. In 1798, the year of rebellion, over 30,000 people were killed in massacres throughout the land. The situation in county Londonderry, in the environs of the Cooke home, was troubled and there was much evidence of rebel activity. His own minister, the Reverend John Glendy, was accused of rebellion and soon emigrated to the United States of America. Henry's own family, however, was loyal which meant an amount of persecution for the Cookes. Henry himself had often to stay away from home and sleep in fields and ditches or in barns or beneath rocks. He witnessed many ugly incidents near home including watching the homes of friends and neighbours being burned and destroyed. These frightening happenings stiffened Henry's resolve to serve God as a minister of the church.

Enrolment at college in Glasgow

Henry was enrolled as a student at Glasgow University in 1802 when he was just 14 years old. There he studied for the Presbyterian ministry. In those days prospective ordinands had to travel to Scotland to study and prepare for their church calling as there were no colleges or training establishments for Presbyterians in Ireland at that time.

Travelling from his home to Glasgow was a most difficult journey. He had to walk 60 miles to Donaghadee in county Down where he boarded the little ferry which crossed the Irish Sea to Portpatrick. Once in Scotland there was nothing else for it but to start walking the entire way to Glasgow, a distance of not much less than 100 miles. The only relief was the fact that, at least, he would not have to travel on his own. Several of his student colleagues had to make the same expedition and so he had company over the many days it took to arrive at college.

He remained there until 1805 by which time he had completed his undergraduate studies. Because of illness he was unable to take his degree although he was still able to preach and carry out his duties as a Presbyterian minister upon his return. However he had learnt much whilst in Glasgow and the experience stood him in good stead for the rest of his life. He even took an elocution class which certainly helped prepare him for his speaking marathons of future life.

An early acquaintance at college was one Henry Montgomery who was to feature strongly in Cooke's later life.

Return to Ireland

When he did come home in 1807 Henry, now licensed to preach, was ordained assistant to the Reverend Robert Scott at Duneane, near Randalstown, in county Antrim. It appears that Henry was not happy with Scott and left to become a tutor after just two years. However he was soon drawn back into the ministry in 1811 when he accepted a call to the congregation at Donegore, also in county Antrim. There he was a very popular and faithful pastor, so much so that they were prepared to allow him time off duty for several months at a time over a period of three years to finally complete his studies.

He was accepted back to Glasgow to undertake further qualifications and remained there for two years before completing these studies in Dublin over a further twelve months. This meant that the Donegore flock were without Henry for very considerable periods in these years. It is possible that he returned over holiday times but the lengthy duration without their minister must have tried the patience of the Donegore people.

And to make matters worse, as far as they were concerned, they soon heard that the congregation in Killyleagh had given Henry a call. He succeeded in attaining the pulpit in county Down and left Donegore in the autumn of 1818. He had barely been seven years in Donegore and this had included the long months and years when he was away in Scotland and Dublin when they had to 'cover' for him. With a heavy heart they bade farewell to Henry Cooke and were exceedingly sorry to see him go.

Arrival in Killyleagh

Henry Cooke was inducted in Killyleagh on 18 September 1818. He was just 30 years old. Almost immediately he discovered that another of the ministers called to preach for the charge was the Reverend Henry Montgomery. Their paths had crossed again. However Montgomery had been offered a teaching post at Belfast's relatively new school, a Presbyterian foundation, the Royal Belfast Academical Institution – known then as now as 'Inst'.

Henry had been appointed to Killyleagh because 'his pulpit power had won the approbation of all'.[1]

Over the next eleven years that Henry Cooke was minister at Killyleagh the whole body of Presbyterianism was blown to and fro in the wind and was buffeted by every sort of disturbance. And Henry Cooke was in the middle of all of this disruption. In fact he caused much of it himself. Yet, at the end of this monumental struggle, the Presbyterian Church in Ireland had survived to take forward the faithful tenets of the church for generations to come.

Old Light and New Light; Arian and Orthodox

There were within the Presbyterian church clergy and people who were described as Arians. They were also called New Light as opposed to the orthodox people being called Old Light. Arians do not believe in the divinity of Christ or in the Holy

Trinity. They believed in God alone and not in Father, Son and Holy Spirit. Most congregations, by the early 19th century, had Arians amongst them as well as orthodox or Trinitarian members. And so it was in Killyleagh.

The 'owner' or landlord in Killyleagh was Mr Archibald Hamilton Rowan of Killyleagh Castle, who had been a founder of the United Irishmen in Dublin whose rebellion had caused so many massacres and deaths in the 1798 rising. The congregation in Killyleagh was mixed although the Arians were in a minority. Their previous minister, the Reverend WD McEwen, had himself been an Arian. However they had agreed to temporarily sink their differences in order to 'land' such an excellent man as Henry Cooke.

But Henry Cooke was diametrically opposed to Arianism. His life's work was to stamp it out and to remove it from mainstream Presbyterianism. He was 'a vigorous champion of orthodoxy and opponent of heresy'.[2] He was anxious to bring all his new congregation in behind him and his chief supporter was Captain Sidney Hamilton Rowan, who was a son of the Arian landlord.

Shortly after Henry became minister at Killyleagh, there arrived in the area, preaching Arianism, the Englishman, the Reverend J Smithurst. This preacher was a renowned advocate of Arianism who had been brought over to Ireland to convert Presbyterians to his view. He addressed huge crowds throughout the country and was invited by Archibald Hamilton Rowan to come to Killyleagh in the spring of 1821. He preached a 'brilliant' sermon to the local congregation and triumphantly challenged Cooke to reply. Henry, however, took the wind out of Smithurst's sails by deferring his reply for a week. This had a twofold purpose – to give himself time to prepare his reply and then to knock his opponent off his guard.

When Henry did respond with a scintillating oration the following Sunday, Smithurst and his supporters acknowledged that they had been soundly defeated. The Arian missionary was then stalked by Henry Cooke throughout county Down until he eventually fled Ireland with his tail between his legs. Henry Cooke had asserted his, and the orthodox church's, authority.

Taking up the cudgels for orthodoxy

Now that the Arian influence had been largely removed from Killyleagh, Cooke turned his attentions to 'Inst' in Belfast. As Ireland did not have its own theological college the plan was for 'Inst' to act as such a college and to prepare many of the young men at the school for the Presbyterian ministry. But the strong influences at the school were Arian and appointments were being made of professors who advocated that stance. This did not, of course, please Henry Cooke. Nor did it please the Presbyterian Synod. But most of the members of that Synod were weak-willed and were not prepared to oppose certain appointments that the school board was making.

One such appointment was that of Dr William Bruce as professor of Greek and Hebrew whose views were unashamedly Arian. It took some time to adequately resolve the issues at the school but, by his determination, Henry Cooke was eventually able to bring the school into line.

It should be noted that, throughout his long career, Henry Cooke had so often to carry on many a lone struggle on issues which were vital to his vision for the future of the Presbyterian Church. Too often his colleagues were lacklustre in their support and were even opposed to him. They knew that Cooke was right but they did not have the courage to follow his example and lead. At length they did but not before Cooke had almost despaired of ever getting their encouragement and support.

In 1824 Henry was rewarded for his endeavours. He was elected Moderator of the Church, an appointment he held twice again in his life, in 1841 and 1862. He even received a call to preach to the Armagh congregation but there were too many local Arians there to give him the call.

Again, in 1824, the Royal Commission on education met over a period of a year. Henry Cooke was interested in the future of children's education in Ireland so he responded with recommendations and suggestions. In due course he was summoned to appear before the commissioners and his views, or many of them, were accepted. However they were opposed by many Arians and by others in positions of influence. This did not faze Cooke. Once more he stood alone yet was eventually vindicated. He had gone to the trouble of making contributions while so many of his so-called well-meaning colleagues had not. They were talkers; Henry Cooke was a doer.

2.
The Major Crisis for Presbyterianism

Each year the clergy and representatives of the laity of the Presbyterian Church met in synod. It was the annual opportunity to discuss pressing church affairs. But the synods of 1827, 1828 and 1829 turned out to be the most critical for the future of the church. The disputes over Arians and their beliefs were coming to a head. Although they were in the minority the Arian clergy and people were influential. Their leader was Henry Montgomery. He was an able man; a talented orator and a feisty opponent of those of the orthodox Presbyterian persuasion. Arians declared that creeds and confessions were unscriptural and man-made formulae. The Bible was their standard of faith.

The stage was set and the sessions at the synods in 1827 and 1828 proved to be disruptive and overbearing. The Arians felt themselves in the ascendancy and the debates and sermons of Montgomery powerfully asserted the Arian cause. The only one to have the will and ability to oppose them was Henry Cooke. He knew he would receive little help from his own side so he made his preparations to deal as many heavy blows as possible against Henry Montgomery. The sermons of both men were comprehensive and lengthy and contained much to cause offence to the opposing speaker.

But Cooke was able for his opponents and succeeded in having a motion passed that would debar clergy who did not strictly adhere to mainstream Presbyterian principles and beliefs. Any minister not preaching the doctrine of the Trinity would be removed from his congregation. It seemed that the Arians were beaten. However they rallied with a grim determination to defeat Cooke and his colleagues at the Lurgan Synod in June 1829.

The greatest confrontations ever to be experienced within the Presbyterian Church took place at this momentous gathering. The chief protagonists were, of course, Cooke and Montgomery. In their three hour debates both men used vitriolic language; accusations abounded and the future of the church seemed on a knife edge. And so it was.

In the end, after further protracted debate and discussion amongst the synod members, the outcome favoured Cooke and the orthodox Presbyterians. Henry Montgomery acknowledged defeat and, with 17 ministers and their congregations, he withdrew from the synod. Thus was formed 'The Remonstrant Synod of Ulster', known as Non Subscribing Presbyterians.

There continued to be bitter disputes between these factions. The Non Subscribing congregations demanded that they held on to their church property and lands and the matter was not finally settled until the passing of an Act of Parliament, The Dissenters Chapels Act of 1844 which, in large measure, did allow the Non Subscribers to hold on to their church buildings.

The church, rather than falling into gloom and lethargy, actually re-awoke. Under the leadership shown by Cooke the Presbyterian Church revived with many new congregations, Sunday Schools and churches and a zeal for missionary work. In Killyleagh these renewed vitalities manifested themselves in the rebuilding of the Church and the increase in the congregation.

Consolidation within the Presbyterian Church

Steps had been initiated to unite the Synod of Ulster and the Secession Synod in 1818 and, by 1836, both sides seemed close to agreement. Union eventually took place in 1840 when 292 General Synod and 141 Secession congregations formed to become the General Assembly of the Presbyterian Church in Ireland. There were now a total of 433 congregations with over 650,000 members. Only eight Secession congregations remained outside the new fold.

Henry Cooke, although still a powerful minister, was not always popular with all Presbyterians as the years went by. He held many maverick views which did not find favour and he was now seldom able to bend the Synod's will as he had done in the past. They often listened to what Cooke had to say and then went their own way.

It appeared, in retrospect, that Henry Cooke's greatest triumph, if such is the correct word, was the purging of Arianism from the church.

But what of life back in Killyleagh?

Whilst the debates raged in the Presbyterian Synod over those critical years of the late 1820s, life went on in Killyleagh. Cooke had the extraordinary capacity to work long hours. Hard work seemed to suit him. So while he prepared his case for debate at Synod, he ensured that his chief attentions remained with his own congregation. He was, after all, their pastor first and a member of Synod second.

In the summer of 1827 a local confrontation over the future of his own congregation occurred. There were still both orthodox and Arian factions within the Killyleagh people. Most obviously there was the difference of opinion between the Hamilton Rowans in the Castle. Mr Archibald favoured Arianism and Captain Sidney orthodoxy. Time would soon tell whether the congregation would remain Trinitarian and orthodox or be persuaded by the Arian point of view.

A lengthy and urgent correspondence between Cooke and Archibald Hamilton Rowan was entered into over the course of just one day. All day long letter after letter was exchanged between Castle and manse. Hamilton Rowan wanted the arguments debated and quickly resolved. The minister, however, wanted the decision to be taken by the session and people of the church. As ever Cooke put his case in a detailed and measured way. The landlord did not fully understand the points being made by Henry Cooke and, in the hope of bringing the matter to a head, took the unusual step of jumping up to address the congregation at the conclusion of the following Sunday morning service.

Cooke, of course, was surprised by Rowan's action but refused to allow him to talk to the people who hurriedly left the church on the advice, and instruction, of their minister. Mr Hamilton Rowan was left standing alone in his pew in the church. His action, probably ill-advised, was the straw which broke the camel's back. Before many days were over the congregation had made its decision. They agreed with their minister that the one main principle was 'the fundamental of Presbyterianism to be the honest exercise of private judgment' and declared themselves truly orthodox. As an immediate consequence the Arians in the congregation left to join groups of like minded individuals elsewhere.

At this time their new church was built with Henry Cooke himself taking much to do with its design and construction. It was a splendid edifice, one which would have fittingly adorned any metropolis. It was a fitting tribute to his reign as minister of the Killyleagh congregation. During his years in the village his influence increased not only amongst his own people but also throughout the country and further afield.

First Killyleagh Presbyterian Church built during Cooke's ministry

At home in Killyleagh he undertook his own version of expelling the moneylenders from the temple. He drove away the women who, every Sunday morning at his own church gates, stood selling sweets to the congregation. He also took the decision to increase the time between Sunday services. Normally morning service was fairly quickly followed by an afternoon service. The reason for this was that some people, especially those who had to travel a distance to church, could have some lunch in Killyleagh and then return to church without having to go home in between times.

However a problem had arisen when the men of the congregation who, instead of lunching with their wives and family between services, headed for the local public houses. As a consequence, therefore, the number attending afternoon service was significantly reduced when the men decided to stay put in the bars. Henry Cooke considered that, if the time span between services was increased, then the men might then return to church. He would, of course, have preached about the problem and shamed the men into returning. Whether or not they did is not entirely clear, but it did mean a much longer day in town for the women and children. It would have been a hollow victory for Dr Cooke.

The Church of Ireland rector in Killyleagh from 1825 was the famous Egyptologist, Dr Edward Hincks and he and Cooke often engaged in debates on matters of theology. They remained good friends throughout their lives as Hincks was a firm believer in Cooke's stance on Presbyterian orthodoxy and an opponent of the Non Subscribers.

Cooke's translation to Belfast

After just eleven years in Killyleagh during the great upheavals in the Presbyterian Church, Henry Cooke was installed as minister of the new May Street Church in Belfast which had been specially built for him. This was a very fine building similar in design to the Killyleagh church. Cooke had taken a hand in the design of his new church too.

The Killyleagh congregation was sorry that he was departing from them for he had won their undying affection and confidence. They also appreciated that Henry Cooke's talents were needed elsewhere and they did not want to stand in his way. He was presented with numerous gifts from a grateful congregation. A great multitude of people gathered to hear Henry Cooke's final sermon in Killyleagh on 8 November 1829.

The great legacy of Dr Henry Cooke

Henry Cooke left Killyleagh when he was just 41 years old and he lived almost another 40 years. Over these subsequent years he continued to be a very prominent churchman. He wrote and edited books and pamphlets and gave guidance to many of the younger men coming into the church. He remained a popular preacher, whose sermons were said to have magic in them, and his services were sought by congregations throughout the length and breadth of the British Isles. He received honours from colleges and universities; he promoted Presbyterian and Protestant ethics and he continued to revel in the cut and thrust of Synod debates.

'Men, not a few, excelled Dr Cooke in writing; men, but few, equalled him in speaking'.[3] He did lend his support for Catholic emancipation and enfranchisement. He gave his support to the beleaguered Church of Ireland as it approached disestablishment. He helped revive Presbyterian congregations when they were in difficulties. Contrary to the views of some Presbyterian and other Protestant churches, Henry Cooke saw the Roman Catholic Church as part of the 'visible' church and did not wish to have converts re-baptised. These stances taken by Cooke were constantly at odds with many other Presbyterian clergy. But he advanced them undeterred.

Henry Cooke was elected Moderator of the church twice again in 1841 and then in 1862. He became a professor at the new Presbyterian Theological College. He was made a Freeman of Dublin in 1839 and many portraits and busts were executed to adorn church and college walls.

He left a worthy legacy not only to the Presbyterian Church in Ireland but also to the great fabric of Irish society. Few clergymen have left such an indelible mark for this country's future generations. His eleven years in Killyleagh coincided with what could be described as the biggest sea change ever to happen in the Presbyterian Church and so he can fittingly be added to the rolls of Killyleagh's most famous sons.

Plaque inside the Cooke Hall

Dr Edward Hincks

1.
Those Brilliant Early Years

When a resident of Killyleagh brings a visitor up to the parish church on Church Hill, they will pass one of those blue circular plaques which gives information about a famous person who has lived in the town in years gone by. In this case they see the name of Dr Edward Hincks who was a renowned Egyptologist. He lived from 1792 until 1866 and was the rector of Killyleagh from 1825 until his death 41 years later.

Most of us appreciate the meaning of what a rector is – priest or minister of the local Church of Ireland church. In Killyleagh's case it is the church of St John the Evangelist, a church originally built in 1640 but radically remodelled in 1812. But what on earth is or was an Egyptologist and what on earth was one doing in the sleepy village of Killyleagh on the shores of Strangford Lough in the middle of the nineteenth century?

This is the story of a most exceptional son of Killyleagh.

The Hincks family

In the early years of the 18th century the Hincks family, who hailed from Chester in England, uprooted themselves and came to live in Ireland. Edward Hincks, along with other families, came over the sea to settle in the south of Ireland, in Cork city. He prospered and married the curiously named Bithia Dix in 1766 and soon had a family of his own.

His son, Thomas Dix Hincks, was a gifted and clever child who, when he had left school, became a Presbyterian minister. This was an unusual occupation in that part of the world as Presbyterians were never numerous in that city. He practised as a minister in Cork for a short time but soon decided to leave the church in order to manage a school of his own in the city, which he did from 1791 until 1803. He was also an officer of the prestigious Royal Cork Institution which prided itself in sending many of its boys to university in Dublin.

He then left Cork to become a tutor at Fermoy College, a town nearly 40 miles north of the city. There he remained from 1815 until 1821 before he made the momentous move to the small town of Belfast in the north east of Ireland. In those days Belfast had not yet become the industrial hub of the island although its population was already beginning to increase.

Thomas Hincks, with his wife, the former Anne Boult also from Chester, and his family made the long and arduous journey by coach and four to Belfast in 1821. That journey would have lasted several very uncomfortable days. The Hinckses had seven children, five sons and two daughters. Edward, their eldest, and the next three sons, William, Thomas and John, all took Holy Orders. Edward and John became Church of Ireland clergymen, whilst William and Thomas became Unitarian ministers. Their youngest son, Francis, also made a name for himself, not in the church but in the diplomatic service and in the field of politics. Sir Francis had a glittering career as Governor of Barbados and then British Guiana and was one time Prime Minister of Canada. Their two daughters, Hannah and Anne, did not seem to achieve much fame at all, typical of the position of women in the early nineteenth century.

Thomas Hincks had come to Belfast to take up a most prestigious post – that of classical headmaster at the Royal Belfast Academical Institution (known as 'Inst'). The school had only newly opened and Hincks helped to shape the institution into the fine educational establishment it is to this day.

His career was further advanced in 1849 when he moved to the new Queen's College in the city to become Professor of Hebrew. By then he was well over 80 years of age. He lived until he was 90 and died in February 1857.

The career of young Edward Hincks

Edward had started his education in Cork at home with tutors engaged to teach him the rudiments of learning. His early years were interrupted in 1798 when the family decided that, owing to the bloody rebellion raging in the southern Irish counties in the summer of that year, it would be best to retreat to England to live near their English relatives. They sailed by ship from Cork to the port of Liverpool which, in those days of sailing ships, was a long and arduous journey. The disruption for the Hincks family was thankfully short-lived, and they returned to Cork at the end of that year.

Young Edward proved to be a bright boy and was then sent to school in Midleton, a town 20 miles east of Cork city. This meant that he had to board, something which did not enthuse him greatly. The school had 60 boarders and around twenty day boys. The masters were eccentric but capable and well-meaning. He enjoyed his schooling there and made many friends.

In 1807 he entered Trinity College in Dublin. He was just 15 years old, a very young age to be sent to university these days, but something which was quite usual back then. He had won first place in the entrance examination and with it a Classical Scholarship. He continued to be a studious young man who regularly won prizes in Greek and mathematics and who graduated with a BA degree and a gold medal five years later in 1812.

Little is known of his days at Trinity, but it seems that he was not a very gregarious young man and did not much care for the Provost at the college. Edward Hincks was gifted and bright and spent most of his time in study and attending lectures. He was also a bit of a loner although he did participate in the activities of a number of the college societies.

It was during his Trinity days that Edward started to take an interest in the dynasties of the Near and Middle East. Whilst there he catalogued a great number of Oriental manuscripts. The age of discovery for the ancient dynasties of the desert regions had arrived and it was clearly a subject which interested the young Hincks. He had been intrigued by what he had read about the Rosetta Stone which had been discovered a few years earlier in Egypt in 1799. His interest had been particularly aroused by its hieroglyphics and the methods used to decipher them. Perhaps, without realising it at the time, he had inadvertently set out on his life's work.

Taking Holy Orders

Like so many young men in those days he decided to take Holy Orders in the Church of Ireland. This would have been a fairly usual step for such a man as Edward Hincks to take. Sons of large families very often chose either a career in the army or navy or in the church. Taking this latter option he successfully completed his training. He was made deacon in 1815 and then priest in 1817, the year he passed his MA degree. This well qualified and gifted young man then found himself appointed as rector of the parish of Ardtrea in the county and diocese of Armagh. He became a popular preacher and was invited to give the sermon in a number of the churches in Armagh diocese and further afield. Some of his sermons were even published such was the quality and excellence of his words from the pulpit.

In February 1823 Edward married Jane Dorothea Boyd and, in due course of time, they had four daughters — Eliza, Anne, Jane and Bithia – the youngest certainly named after her maternal great grandmother. Only one of them, Jane, was to marry which meant that the three others remained with their parents throughout their lives. They were to prove to be quite a financial burden to their father in years to come.

During his time in Ardtrea, Edward, in furtherance of his earlier Oriental studies, began to take a keen interest in reading inscriptions. These were the hieroglyphics depicted on the artefacts which were being regularly unearthed in the deserts of the Near East, in Arabia and Iraq. There were few experts in this field of study and someone had to learn to read them if the ways of the ancient civilisations were to be understood. Edward Hincks seized his opportunity and decided to pursue this hobby, which was to become his great and learned profession. He had taken his first step in achieving prominence in this exciting field of discovery.

In 1825 Edward was appointed to the parish of Killyleagh in county Down in the diocese of Down, Dromore and Connor. He accepted the living with an annual stipend of £795 per annum, £5 less than he had earned in Ardtrea. He was to remain as rector there for the remaining 41 years of his life.

As a churchman, Edward Hincks was a liberal. As such he was usually in the minority amongst his fellow churchmen. He supported Catholic emancipation which was, most definitely, a very unpopular stance to take. Whilst he strongly opposed the doctrines of the Roman Catholic Church, he nonetheless believed that they should have as many civil rights as Protestants. In the middle years of the century, when revivalism and evangelicalism had gripped both the Church of Ireland and the Presbyterian churches, Edward showed his opposition to their popularity and promoted the moderate tenets of his church. Edward Hincks remained an unpopular clerical colleague and found no favour with the now revitalised Orange Order.

Edward Hincks had a social conscience as well. He was keen on education and had a great input into the local schools in Killyleagh. He was also involved in a loan society to help his parishioners and, whilst this did not take off as he wished it to, it did show a compassion strangely absent from many of his fellow churchmen. It has been said that these unpopular campaigns prevented him gaining promotion in his church. He remained a lowly rector throughout his career in the priesthood. No canon's stall in Down Cathedral ever came the way of the Reverend Doctor Edward Hincks who had even become a Doctor of Divinity in 1829.

Perhaps the most unusual support he gave was to those who advocated a change to decimal currency throughout Great Britain and Ireland. Had he succeeded in his endeavours this country would have taken that imaginative step an impressive 120 years prior to its actual realisation.

Another unusual interest of Edward's was playing chess games by correspondence. He spent over six months completing such a game in 1850. In this day and age it is difficult to imagine this process. Each player had a chessboard in front of them and each, in turn, decided what move to make. Each would then write a letter informing his opponent of the move; it would then be posted and the reply patiently awaited. Then the procedure would start all over again with perhaps for as many as 40 moves to make to complete the game.

Lest Edward Hincks be accused of only showing an interest in his Oriental studies, and not in his parishioners, it would be best to acknowledge his passion for social history. In his diary which he commenced in 1848 and wrote right up until his death 18 years later, he mentions amongst other things the 1848 Young Irelanders Rising in Ireland; the revolts in Vienna, which information he received from one of his many correspondents; the struggles in the Crimean War and the arrival of steam railways in England (very soon to be followed in Ireland itself).

An early interest in Hebrew and Eastern languages

Edward Hincks will be remembered, however, not for his duties as rector of Killyleagh, but for his sparkling career as an Egyptologist and an expert in deciphering Near Eastern languages. His first priority was to be a faithful pastor to his people in Killyleagh and this remained his chief aim in life.

But Killyleagh, during his years there, was never a big parish and it made few demands on its rector. He dutifully led the offices of Matins, Evensong and the Holy Eucharist Sunday by Sunday and delivered his weekly sermon. He visited his flock and performed baptisms, weddings and funerals as required of him by his Bishop. He regularly attended select vestry meetings and other gatherings of his congregation. No one could ever point a finger at the good rector of Killyleagh for not carrying out his Godly duties, although, in his later days, he did become somewhat absentminded and was known to pass his parishioners on the street without even acknowledging their presence or answering their friendly salutations. He was even known to leave the pulpit in the middle of his sermon to rush back to the rectory to note down some brainwave about a deciphering problem he had been having. Once he had written down the solution, he returned to church to his long-suffering and patient congregation to finish his address.

By the time he had arrived in Killyleagh from county Armagh Edward Hincks owned a most comprehensive library of books mainly on subjects relating to Egypt and the Near East. He had, by this time, a good knowledge of Arabic and, in 1832, he had written a book on the Egyptian and Hebrew languages and grammar. He also had an enthusiasm for astronomical studies. He was practically alone in his expertise in Ireland at that time and, for that matter, this was to remain the case for the rest of his life.

But Doctor Hincks' greatest and most absorbing hobby meant little to his people and he had plenty of time to devote to its pursuance. They knew he had an interest in ancient Egyptian hieroglyphics but for years they had no real understanding of what this entailed. Edward Hincks' enthusiasm for these esoteric curiosities had been sparked, as we have already noted, whilst he was a student at Trinity. He discovered that he could appreciate the finer points of reading Egyptian papyri which had been brought to Dublin. A seminal paper of his on the subject – 'On the years and cycles of the Egyptians' – was read in Dublin in 1838. A catalogue of Egyptian papyri, with Edward taking a lead role, was published in Dublin in 1840. Scholars from many parts of the world were keeping in close contact with him for advice and guidance in their studies and discoveries. But there were very few of his clerical colleagues who had any inclination to take an interest in such obscure revelations.

There were, however, in different parts of the world other experts in the fields which interested Edward. In the 1820s, in his early days of involvement in hieroglyphics, he made friends, through correspondence, with Jean-François Champollion who also was a decipherer. Both men had made important discoveries in their translations but, even in those early days, it was the work of Edward Hincks which made the headlines. It must never be forgotten that he undertook the vast majority of his work in the rectory study in Killyleagh either with copies of artefacts or from having items actually brought to him.

These circumstances were all the more remarkable since people like Champollion were actually present at the sites in Iran and Mesopotamia. Hincks never had the opportunity to visit the great desert sites and, being remote on the shores of Strangford Lough in a sleepy village in county Down, naturally kept him out of the limelight.

Difficulties for the Doctor Hincks

Hincks was undoubtedly a brilliant man. But he was also a relatively poor man. His salary as rector of Killyleagh was barely adequate especially when he had a large family to look after. He had very little extra money to devote to his hobby. Yet he realised that the discoveries he was making were not only of benefit to him but, more importantly, were of considerable interest to the nation. He was the best in his field.

Consequently he took the incredible step of writing to no less a personage than Sir Robert Peel, the Prime Minister in the early 1840s. He appealed for funding to help him in the groundbreaking work he was pursuing. He hardly needed to point out to Peel the importance of the discoveries that he, Hincks, was making. And these findings were keeping the United Kingdom in the forefront of world Oriental discoveries. But Hincks was to be disappointed as Peel felt unable to give him any assistance. It seemed niggardly of the Prime Minister not to arrange for a small pension to be given to the world leader in the field of Egyptology. One could have understood if Hincks had simply abandoned his efforts and retreated to his flock in Killyleagh. Edward Hincks, however, was made of sterner stuff. His zeal drove him on.

Having been rebuffed Hincks simply moved on. There was so much to do and so little time to do it. He was being invited to give lectures in local towns as well as in Belfast and Dublin. In 1844 he gave a lecture in the neighbouring county town of Downpatrick. There was a Mechanic's Institute there and it was at this venue that Dr Hincks came to talk on 'The Ancient Egyptian Language'. The audience was held spellbound as Hincks explained the importance of this language and enthralled them in discussions about all the various methods he had used to make sense of this ancient civilisation. He was in his element and particularly pleased to be talking to local townspeople. The citizens of these nearby county Down towns realised what a special person they had as a neighbour from Killyleagh and they were indeed proud of him.

He sometimes gave lectures in his own village. On a number of occasions in the early 1850s he delivered such talks as 'The Literature of Ancient Assyria' to the local townspeople in the Courthouse. One wonders what size of an audience would attend such a lecture in Killyleagh in the early years of the twenty first century.

Hincks, at this stage in his career, was well known to many professors at different universities and he encouraged them to teach the ancient languages to their students. He had considerable success and courses burgeoned throughout the length and breadth of the British Isles.

Hincks' enthusiasm for his subjects was infectious. The rector of Killyleagh was in receipt of voluminous correspondence from every part of the world. His views were being sought from the explorers who were often on site with their latest discoveries. As they sat in the sands of the Middle Eastern deserts amidst their newly found tablets and fabulous excavations, they were writing to Hincks in Killyleagh looking for his advices and views on what they might have found. Edward Hincks was the expert yet he never once stood on the sands of Arabia to examine artefacts first hand. The information, the copies and the objects had to be sent to Ireland to Hincks in Killyleagh and the explorers had to wait for their answers as they discovered yet more ancient and priceless artefacts.

In thinking about this amazing situation we can only but appreciate the utterly incredible brilliance of the rector of Killyleagh.

2.
Hincks and his Greatest Discovery

It is important to offer some clear explanations as to what Edward Hincks studied and also how important his discoveries were to civilisation in the mid nineteenth century and beyond. The words used in describing Hincks' great finds (e.g. decipherment, cuneiform, Assyriology) could easily turn the reader off. It is necessary to try to define as many of the words in the vocabulary of Edward Hincks to make sense of his importance to society and especially to let Killyleagh people understand that, although Hincks' hobby was a very specialised one, it was vitally important to the world of science as a whole. We may not understand how man got to the moon, but we do appreciate just how important the event was for the future of mankind. So it is with Edward Hincks and his discoveries. We may not understand his reasons for reading ancient languages, but we may now begin to appreciate just how essential his discoveries were – both to people in Killyleagh and to the wider world.

The decipherment of Mesopotamian Cuneiform

First and foremost Edward Hincks was an Egyptologist. He was a student of the language, history and culture of ancient Egypt. To pursue this interest most people would have visited the regions of the world where the language was spoken – in this case Egypt and the countries of the Near East such as Arabia and Iran. In Hincks' case, because of his vocation as a clergyman, he was never able to go abroad. Yet he was the foremost Egyptologist of his time.

It is interesting to note that Hincks was, as well as one who studied Egyptian hieroglyphics, an able linguist. He had already written a Hebrew grammar book and could speak a number of little known languages like Sanskrit. He was completely at home in Latin and Greek. He was quite simply a most intelligent man.

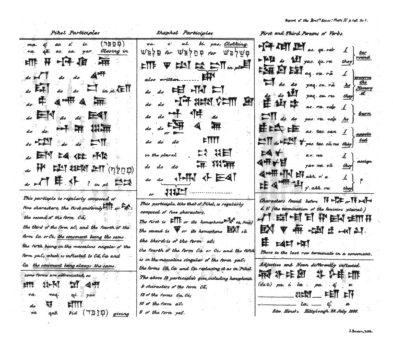

An example of Mesopotamian Cuneiform

By the 1830s, in the early part of Hincks' career, he had turned his attention to cuneiform. A civilisation called the Sumerians, who were the people of ancient Babylon, started using this form of writing perhaps six centuries ago. Their type of script (rather than using papyrus for example) was to write in pictograms, which is the use of pictures or pictorial symbols to communicate their thoughts in physical form. These symbols were written on vertical stone columns and tablets. The signs or symbols were wedge shaped characters and these were called cuneiform signs. So it was that these pictorial cuneiform signs became the basis of their language.

These cuneiform tablets were fired in a kiln and so became a permanent record. Being so hard they were difficult and almost impossible to destroy. Even when great civilisations were burned down, the tablets remained, perhaps undetected, but relatively undamaged.

Once these tablets were discovered in the Near East they were brought (or the information copied) to Edward Hincks at the rectory in Killyleagh. One of the most crucial jobs in the translation of these ancient signs was that of the copier. Many of the artefacts could not be physically removed from their sites, so someone had to copy them. These men meticulously and painstakingly followed the lines and indentations and copied them on to paper to send back to Killyleagh for Edward Hincks to decipher. There were good copiers and bad ones. Thankfully most were in the former category and Hincks rarely had any complaints. The skill of the cuneiform copyist was vital.

One can only wonder what the postmen of his day thought of the large and bulky parcels that had to be delivered to him from all the exotic outposts of the then known world. Many of these rare items were brought by ship to the harbour in Killyleagh and then transported to the rectory by horse and cart. It was fortunate that the rectory in Killyleagh was a very large building, big enough to hold the artefacts arriving from foreign lands. Presumably, too, his wife and daughters learned to take no notice of the strange objects which festooned the rectory floors.

Life in the rectory for Mrs Hincks and her daughters had to carry on regardless of Dr Hincks' hobby. Mrs Hincks' health was never robust and it must have been a struggle for her to keep body and soul together for herself and the family including, of course, Edward himself. Their daughters, despite their father's eccentricities, did their best to enjoy life in Killyleagh attending dances, picnics, writing for magazines and playing charades. There was always plenty going on in the village.

Edward Hincks was equal to the task. After years spent in discovering the meaning of the cuneiform signs he was able to read the tablets with a fair degree of ease. His skill at deciphering was remarkable and, whilst he was not the trailblazer in discovering cuneiform, he certainly streaked ahead of all his colleagues and rivals in answering the question – and what does this tablet say? It was often Hincks who was the first to give the answer.

Hincks – his friends and his rivals

Throughout his sparkling career Edward Hincks regularly locked horns with other Egyptologists and scientists. He was skilful and thorough in everything he attempted. He made many friends in his field as well as many who were his undoubted rivals. One of the men with whom Hincks often crossed swords was Colonel (later Sir) Henry Rawlinson who was in the British Army and usually stationed in areas where excavations were taking place. There was an intense rivalry between the two men and, although they respected each other's particular skills, there were often times when they did not see eye to eye.

Rawlinson was, in truth, a great explorer. He made an outstanding discovery in Persia in 1835 where thousands of cuneiform signs were unearthed. Rawlinson knew that it would be Hincks who could read these signs before he could and as ever, although he had by far the greatest opportunities to make progress himself at the very site of the discovery, he had to swallow his pride and send the tablets to Hincks. It does not mean that Rawlinson had no skills of his own – he certainly had – but he possessed much less patience than Hincks and it was endurance that was needed to decipher the fabulous tablets. Too often his jealousy of Hincks was an unnecessary obstacle in the pursuit of excellence in the mastery of cuneiform.

The fact that Hincks was alone in his rectory with the tablets without the distractions experienced by Rawlinson in the field probably allowed him to concentrate on the matter in hand. He was dealing with one treasure at a time and his incisiveness was put to good use as he methodically examined and deciphered the latest finds from the desert. There were rather too often mistakes made by Rawlinson which Hincks had to rectify. The Englishman tended to be an inaccurate or even a careless translator and this slovenliness of Rawlinson too often distracted Hincks from his work. Sadly Rawlinson failed to acknowledge Hincks' findings and quotations in books which he wrote. This attitude forced scientists to take sides and, whilst many were admirers of Rawlinson, the clear majority would have taken the side of Hincks. However this support was not enough to change Rawlinson's mind when it came to acknowledging fairly Hincks' own findings.

Hincks and Rawlinson did meet, probably on one of Edward's visits to England in the earlier days. As the years passed by and Rawlinson's craftiness increased, Edward realised that his rival, being the kind of bombastic and cunning man that he was, would continue to take credit for work he had done. There were stages in Edward's life when he became despondent sometimes even threatening to give up altogether. In the vast correspondence between Hincks and his colleagues, the name of Henry Rawlinson was ever present. Few were satisfied at the way his rival was proceeding. It was rather a case of Rawlinson tramping over everyone else.

One of Edward Hincks' greatest friends was the French archaeologist, Paul Emile Botta. They were both skilful in reading ancient Assyrian and Babylonian cuneiforms. Luck was with Hincks in 1842 when Botta made the remarkable discovery of the ancient city of Nineveh. This was possibly the greatest archaeological find of the nineteenth century. Apart from finding tens of thousands of baked clay tablets with cuneiform signs, Botta had unearthed the great library of Assurbanipal which also contained thousands of cuneiform inscriptions. It must have been an earth-shattering experience for the Frenchman but, for Hincks, in faraway Killyleagh, the opportunities were endless. The postal traffic from the desert to Ireland in those years must have been tremendous. The discoveries made by Hincks were clearly overwhelming and exceptional.

Hincks had, by now, completely honed his skills in cuneiform, but he also continued to improve his deciphering abilities in reading the Old Persian and Elamite languages. His correspondence with luminaries in various universities throughout the British Isles and in Europe assisted professors there to further elucidate the languages of the ancient civilisations. Hincks' reports and lecture notes, which were often many pages long, were sought after for years to come.

In 1847, by which time he was 55 years old, Hincks paid a visit to Oxford. It was his first time there and he was at last able to mix with those men who had influenced him and who, in turn, had also been inspired by Hincks. His advices were continually being sought – something which greatly pleased Hincks. According to so many eminent men Edward Hincks was 'the fountain of all knowledge'. This fact was indisputable. He felt that his days spent in the study in Killyleagh had been worthwhile. The country parson's name was famous and respected in places of importance.

After he had returned from Oxford, where he would have stayed for a few weeks, he was again in the public eye. The local newspapers would have been proud to note that Dr Hincks had been sought after in such learned places as the old university city of Oxford. His own congregation in Killyleagh would have missed their rector and would have been served, in those weeks, by other clergy from the diocese.

In 1848 the Royal Irish Academy awarded Edward the Cunningham Medal for his research into Egyptian hieroglyphics. This was an acknowledgement of the respect in which Hincks was held in the academic world not only in Ireland but throughout Europe. His scholarly papers, regularly published and printed at Trinity, were evidence, if such was needed, of his magnificent contribution to the sciences.

In 1850 he was invited to lecture to the Belfast Natural History and Philosophical Society. His subject was Assyrian inscriptions, a topic on which he truly excelled. His large and learned audience was transfixed by what they heard for they realised that they were in the presence of probably the greatest Assyriologist in the world.

Many of the same people would have returned to Belfast later that year in October to attend the unrolling of two

Egyptian mummies which had been specifically brought to Ireland from Luxor by the world famous Sir James Tennant. Prominent at Tennant's side that night was that other Egyptologist of note, Dr Edward Hincks. It must have been an honour not only to Ireland but also to Hincks that Tennant had decided to bring two such wonderful finds to Belfast to unroll. He could easily have chosen a seat of learning in England but he obviously felt that Ireland, and Hincks, should be the first to view these rare and outstanding discoveries.

Hincks was invited to unroll other mummies in Liverpool, for example, but it is uncertain whether or not he was able to attend. His expertise was regularly sought as evidenced in a letter from Mr Edward Clibborn from the Royal Irish Academy about some markings on a mummy which elicited this comment – 'should you enlighten our darkness as to the import of the hieroglyphics sent, we shall be much obliged'.[1]

Edward Hincks had a great friend in the field of Egyptology and science, Dr Austen Layard. Both men respected each other and were regularly in contact. Hincks had a great affinity with Layard especially as he seemed to be a discreet and tactful man and one who never failed to show his indebtedness for all the help that the Irishman had given him. Like Hincks Layard had been 'stung' by Rawlinson and so they had a mutual suspicion of the Englishman. Hincks was able to unburden himself on Layard and, in the early 1860s, was very anxious for Layard to come over to spend time with him at the rectory in Killyleagh. There were many matters of importance which Hincks wanted to discuss with his dear friend and his letters to him for many months concerned the dates when he would travel to Ireland.

In the end Layard did come for two weeks in September 1852 but, in considering the length of correspondence, one wonders why it took Layard so long to get over to see his Irish friend. One could perhaps surmise that Layard found the prospect of the journey across the Irish Sea too daunting or maybe he felt that time spent in the wilds of county Down would be nugatory and not entirely worthwhile. But this is probably being unfair to Layard and, whilst at the Killyleagh rectory, both men wasted no time in examining recent inscriptions sent to Edward.

Gloom and despondency

Edward Hincks fell into obscurity at various stages of his life. He lived in Ireland, far away from the hub of scientific interest; he did not hold an academic post in an English university; he was rarely able to travel to London or other English cities to deliver his addresses. This was mainly because he could neither afford the time away from his priestly duties nor the expenditure for the journey. One of the most galling difficulties for Hincks was not being able to present his own lectures. He had to rely on someone else reading them to an audience which would have gained so much more had it been Hincks himself addressing them. For such a prominent and noteworthy man such as Edward Hincks not to be in a position to deliver his own lectures must have been the worst possible indignity. This, however, was the stark reality for this wonderful and learned man. There was little he could do. The world hung on his every word yet it seemed unable to improve the lot of its master.

This despondency is epitomised in the words of Lady Dufferin who, as Lady Hariot Rowan Hamilton from Killyleagh Castle, had been married by Dr Hincks himself in 1862 in a room in the castle. Even she, who had lived in Killyleagh and who had been one of Edward's parishioners, had never appreciated her own rector's worth in the world of cuneiform and hieroglyphics until after his death. 'I am afraid that I did not realise till afterwards that he was a celebrated man, and of course he should not have been confined to a little country parish, but should have been in the society of other learned men, and have had complete leisure for his investigations, in the atmosphere of some great university'.[2]

3.
The Height of Hincks' Career

By 1850 Hincks was at the height of his career. His name was known throughout the world and his advices were regularly sought by other scientists and Egyptologists. He was undertaking more and more translations of hieroglyphics and his fame went before him. And still he remained in his rectory in Killyleagh. The world expert was but a lowly church parson making discoveries which were to affect the entire world of antiquarianism whilst taking time out to prepare his weekly sermons to deliver from the pulpit in St John's church every Sunday to his faithful congregation.

His finances were still in a critical situation. Rather than receiving an ever increasing salary, his income was in fact reducing. He had tried, always unsuccessfully, to gain promotion in the Church of Ireland. The dean's position in Armagh had been vacant at a time but another clergyman had been favoured over Edward Hincks. By age 60 he knew that his chances of moving from Killyleagh were minimal. There were many who thought that this 'most learned man in Ireland' should be appointed a bishop never mind to any lesser position. Their views, too, fell on deaf ears.

He took the unusual step of writing to his English friends to discover whether or not there was a vacant sinecure English parish available. He thought that, if he had a parish within easy striking distance of London, he could probably be given a post even at the British Museum. But he was just as unsuccessful in this endeavour as he had been in his own diocese. He was even prepared to resign his clerical living if a professorship might be offered to him. This seemed an intolerable position for such a scholarly man.

His friend, Austen Layard, appreciated Hincks' dire predicament. He understood, perhaps better than anyone, the unfairness experienced by his friend. So he wrote to the Trustees of the British Museum. He, of course, realised the incongruity of approaching the Museum for Edward Hincks since it had been another son of Killyleagh, Sir Hans Sloane, who had founded that very museum. It was almost as if Layard was acting as a mediator between two men who had lived in the same county Down village, seeking justice from one for the other.

Layard recommended to the haughty trustees that Dr Hincks should be employed to read a number of Assyrian tablets which were as yet unread at the Museum. Hincks could also superintend a number of displays which needed attention within its hallowed halls. Hincks was eventually given the job, firstly for three months from February to April 1853, and then on a year's contract from May 1853. He was paid the miserly sum of £120 for his year's work. He even had to stay in lodgings to make ends meet. What happened in Killyleagh during his absence is unknown although one would expect that his family remained there and substitute clergy held the fort until the rector returned in 1854.

The report of his year's work at the British Museum was ready by April 1854. It was of the highest importance especially to the Museum. The government, in the guise of the Lord Lieutenant at Dublin Castle, had realised the excellent work Hincks had done on behalf of the nation and decided to award him an annual pension in recompense for services rendered. It was for the paltry sum of £100 per annum. This derisory allowance made to the most famous Egyptologist of his generation for vital work carried out was the best a grateful nation could afford. In the words of the eminent Egyptologist, Edwin Norris, – 'I feel ashamed for my country, which thus scandalously neglects the claims of such genius and learning'.[3]

Hincks, naturally enough, remained suspicious of the motives of the British Museum staff. They were only too keen to take the credit for the work carried out by him, doing their best to claim the findings as their own. They were never averse to 'doing down' Dr Hincks. His paranoia was well founded as a number of acknowledgements for his work had been wrongly and mischievously declared as their own. His entreaties to ensure that the findings were published were also unfulfilled.

And, as ever, the jealous Rawlinson was hovering in the wings to take credit for discoveries of Edward Hincks.

Hincks, however, did not let the Museum away with their indiscretions. In 1857 he submitted a memorial to them insisting that they fully acknowledged work that was his. He had had too much of their sleights of hand. He also ensured that his findings and exhibits placed in the Museum were forever accessible to the public. This public spirited attitude to the viewing of his discoveries clearly mirrors the similar stand taken by his fellow son of Killyleagh, Sir Hans Sloane, who always had ensured that his artefacts belonged as much to the members of the public as to the great Museum.

In 1857 a number of significant Assyrian inscriptions had been found which needed to be deciphered. It was decided that the four leading orientalist experts should be asked to translate the tablets. The eminent English Egyptologist, Fox Talbot, was invited to join the so-called 'Holy Trinity of cuneiform' – Hincks, Rawlinson and the German, Oppert, to undertake the work. A jury of experts was to sit and pass judgment on the findings of the four men. Copies of the cuneiforms were sent to them and, in due course, the results were examined to decide which were the most accurate translations. Those of Hincks and Rawlinson were adjudged the most precise with Hincks coming out just on top because it was he who was asked to write the memorial. The outcome of these examinations led to the judgement that the decipherment of cuneiform was now a fait accompli.

His crowning years

Edward Hincks was a man of correspondence. His postman delivering his mail each day at the rectory must have been amazed at the postmarks on the many and varied parcels and letters which he had to deliver. Writing to people was the only way for him to keep in touch with the world of Egyptology. As often as he could he had published his articles in journals and magazines. His writings were sought after by a myriad of interested scientists.

In 1859 he got to know Professor Peter Le Page Renouf who was a Guernseyman and professor of Ancient History and Oriental Languages at the Catholic University in Dublin. He was the sole holder of such an appointment in the British Isles. Renouf, of course, realised what a scholar Hincks was and the two cultivated their friendship for the remaining years of Hincks' life. At the same time it seems certain that Trinity clearly missed the golden opportunity to appoint Edward Hincks as Professor in the field of cuneiform and hieroglyphics. Had they done so their name and reputation would have been further greatly enhanced.

He did receive a number of acclamations in his later years. The King of Prussia, for example, appointed him as a Chevalier of Prussia. Edward was in good company – other recipients of this title included the composer, Liszt, and Sir Henry Rawlinson who, for all his craftiness, accomplished enough to receive this accolade. He had been enrolled, in 1856, as an Honorary Member of the Royal Asiatic Society although, it was rumoured, Edward himself had not been keen to be elected.

Hincks took ill with jaundice around Christmas 1863 and, for the greater part of 1864, correspondence abruptly stopped. He still received mail but was unable to answer it. He went to Harrogate in England to recuperate throughout the summer of 1864 and his health improved in consequence of the time spent there.

His entire family was saddened by the death, from yellow fever, of his nephew, Edward, the son of his Governor brother, Sir Francis. The young man had just graduated and was on a visit to the West Indies to see his father. Hincks had to comfort his family and try to fathom the reason for the death of such a fine and able nephew and son.

Edward Hincks was working on an Assyrian grammar and dictionary at the end of 1866 when he suddenly and peacefully died on 3 December at the rectory. He was 74 years old and his loss was deeply felt by the rectory family, the parishioners of Killyleagh and by the entire world of Egyptology and science. He was buried in the churchyard and a memorial adorns the church itself by way of a plaque under the east window. His archdeacon brother, John, in his funeral oration, appealed to the congregation never to forget the contribution made by their excellent rector.

In 1904, 38 years after Hincks' death, an article appeared in the Belfast newspaper, the News Letter, appealing to its readers to send a photograph of Dr Hincks because a bust was to be made of him for the new museum in Cairo, Egypt. One of his daughters responded and the photograph was sent to the young 23 year old Frenchman, Xavier Barthe, who executed the work and it still, to this day, adorns the halls of that great museum.

At the time of the centenary of his death in 1966, the blue plaque was erected on the wall alongside the building that was the rectory until the latter part of the twentieth century.

4.
The Legacy of Edward Hincks

'The place of Edward Hincks in history is secure; it is he, and he almost alone, who made it possible to read once again the memorials of the world's civilisation'.[4] 'He gave Irish Egyptology a brilliant beginning'.[5] 'He was a linguist of considerable distinction'.[6]

Edward Hincks never attained in his lifetime the honour due to his name. Even in subsequent decades right up to the present day, he is only remembered by a very few. It is even sadder to say that the people of Killyleagh itself have forgotten, if they had ever known about, this brilliant man. In the middle of the nineteenth century half way through Queen Victoria's long reign, most of the world's scholars regularly corresponded with him. They appreciated that his achievements were impressive and that his contributions to the ancient languages were extraordinary.

Yet this excellent man rarely left his humble rectory in county Down despite his achievements and expertise; he was often despondent and depressed; he was never honoured by the monarch; there were no great biographies written about him. He fell into obscurity even during his lifetime; his lack of self esteem was even expressed in his own miniscule handwriting. He was destined for the gloom and shadows of the world when he should have been the shining light. Even his greatest revelations in the field of Egyptology and Assyriology were too often misrepresented by people like Rawlinson and the Trustees at the British Museum who rather considered that Edward Hincks was beneath them. Jealousy raged when every chance should have been grasped to lead the country untrammelled into the forefront of the world of cuneiform and decipherment where it belonged.

There were detractors from this viewpoint, of course. Supporters of Henry Rawlinson would say that it was he who triumphed in deciphering the ancient languages overcoming his brilliant, but bitter, rival Edward Hincks. Others described the rivalry between the two men as both poignant and appalling especially considering that, between them, they had solved the puzzle of cuneiform and unravelled the ancient languages. One reviewer described the rivalry as 'being pretty sad really'. This rather epitomises the situation. Whilst it is probably correct in saying that Hincks usually had the edge over Rawlinson, nonetheless both men opened up so many new discoveries in this ancient art which could very easily have remained undiscovered and unexplained for centuries to come.

Throughout his life Edward Hincks was unfairly treated. When the government had the opportunity to recompense him, they failed to grasp it; when the Church of Ireland had the chance to promote such a learned and virtuous cleric, they missed their opening; when the Killyleagh-founded British Museum had the golden opportunity to honour and utilise the talents of yet another of the village's sons, they showed their innate prejudice against this worthy Irishman and took no action. Perhaps it was because he was an Irishman, living in the wilds of a country out of favour with Great Britain, that Hincks was conveniently forgotten. Discoveries of ancient civilisations and the reading of cuneiform signs – for all their wonderment – took a back seat in the midst of the all-consuming problems of Ireland's struggles over Catholic emancipation, the shame of yet another abortive rebellion and the horrors of the Great Famine and the ensuing scandals surrounding the myths of emigration.

Edward Hincks was a perfectionist. It was his chief endeavour in deciphering a language to discover the rules of grammar. For others this approach was not exciting or, in today's parlance, 'sexy' enough. Verbs and nouns and sentence construction were dull and tedious; the really attention-grabbing and fabulous signs and monuments in the deserts of Arabia were much more appealing to the general public.

He was never afraid to constructively criticise or be criticised. He never took the line of least resistance. Hincks, however, stuck to his thorough translations and it was he, and no one else, who understood what the true fundamentals of a language were. His accuracy and meticulous care in his attention to detail ensured the completion of one of the greatest studies ever undertaken of the ancient languages of the world.

His principal direction throughout his life had been the discovery of the truth and he never had any thought of his own personal reputation.

Edward Hincks, the rector of Killyleagh, has left a legacy of which the people of Killyleagh should be proud. It behoves them now not to forget him.

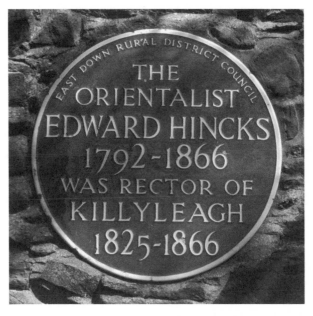

The blue plaque on Church Hill, Killyleagh

Terry Cochrane

1.
The Early Years

I can count myself most fortunate for I knew Terry Cochrane as a young man. When I first came to live near Killyleagh in the late 1960s I became Scoutleader of the Scout Troop at the Parish church in Killyleagh early in 1968. Terry was a member of the Troop when I arrived – and a very keen one too. A large part of Scouting involved mixing with other Scouts in the area and football was always popular at Scout camp and at weekends. There began in those days a District Scout Football competition which our Killyleagh Parish Troop won for the first year or two.

And our chief striker was none other than Terry Cochrane himself.

I have many happy memories of watching the wonderful skill of the young man as he ran rings round the opposition either to score himself or to pass the ball for a friend to sink the ball into the back of the net. The lads, with Terry in charge, were unbeatable and our Troop was the envy of all our other district colleagues. In the spring of 1969 the boys went to

Terry, and the Killyleagh Parish Scouts, receiving the Northern Ireland Scout Football Cup from NI international Bryan Hamilton, May 1969

Crawfordsburn to play in the Northern Ireland Scout 5-a-side Championships. The winners, almost inevitably since Terry was captain of the team, were Killyleagh. Terry and his team, who were pretty good players themselves let it be said, were presented with the cup by the Northern Ireland international, Bryan Hamilton.

One of my abiding memories of Terry Cochrane in the Scouts was when he and the lads were playing football at summer camp at Gilwell Park in London in 1969. When some of the local English Scouts challenged Killyleagh to a football match, they thought it would be a stroll. But they had not reckoned with the Northern Irish boys having Terry Cochrane in their team. They were, of course, soundly thrashed, and disappeared with their tails between their legs. They had more than met their match.

And what was just as thrilling was that later that same day – 21 July 1969 – man landed on the moon. As the boys relaxed after their football match beside the swimming pool, their camp duties behind them, they strained to hear those memorable words emitting from their crackly radio when Neil Armstrong declared — 'That's one small step for a man, one giant leap for mankind'. Terry and I will always be able to remember where we were when Armstrong landed on the moon.

Terry's early life

William John and Teresa Cochrane had six children; three daughters, Margaret, June and Joan and three sons, Hugh, Noel and Terry. Terry was born in Killyleagh on 23 January 1953 the second youngest of the Cochrane family. They lived close to the shore on Cuan Beach not far from the village's harbour where coal boats were regularly to be seen discharging their cargoes on the quay. At the end of their road, on the other side of the harbour, was the Killyleagh Yacht Club. Sailing was, and still is, a very popular activity in Killyleagh. Its favourable position is said to make it one of the best of the dozen or more sailing clubs around the shores of the lovely and picturesque Strangford Lough.

For the children of Killyleagh in those days the primary school, properly known as Killyleagh Primary School but better know to all and sundry as the 'White' school, was Terry's first place of learning. There he spent his early years playing football with the other youngsters in the school playground. In 1964 he moved to Killyleagh High School, very close to his Cuan Beach home. It didn't take long to get up to school so sleeping in was not ever a real concern. Two minutes would have taken him up to school if he had ignored the morning wake up call from his mother.

The High school was never very large. There may have been 200 pupils at the most and there Terry enjoyed his lessons – or at least as much as a teenager would. He excelled in his school days, not so much at football, but at cross country running. He won the school championship twice and came runner up on two other occasions. In his last year at school he won the Northern Ireland inter schools championship.

You may be surprised to learn that football was not Terry's number one school sport. It may have been his own favourite sport but to his Physical Education teacher, Eric Gourlay, Terry wasn't much of a footballer. He only ever made up the school team if Mr Gourlay was having difficulties in finding enough players. In later life, Gourlay was reputed to have been surprised and dumbfounded to hear that Terry Cochrane had become a professional player.

Back at home, however, Terry was playing out his dreams of becoming that selfsame professional football player. At every opportunity he was playing with his friends, Tom Healy, Trevor Rea, Clifford and Malcolm Healy, Gary Watson, Peter Scott and his brother, Hugh. Their favourite venue for their matches was at the square beside the quay end where they all must have been skilful enough to prevent the ball from falling into the tide – although one feels sure it must have done so from time to time. The lads played all day and all night on that quay surrounded by mammoth piles of coal and other sundry equipment found at the harbour. It may have just been a concrete harbour pitch but to Terry and his friends it was their field of football dreams.

As a boy Terry was a great supporter of Tottenham Hotspur although his brother, Hugh, favoured Manchester United, one of whose stars in those days was the legendary George Best. The boys collected all sorts of football memorabilia and knew the name of every player who played in the English First Division. Football was already in Terry's blood. He was surely on his way to the top.

The opening shots in a dazzling football career

Terry's early days at dribbling around opponents and shooting at goal were down at the quay in Killyleagh or playing against the wall of his house with his brother at Cuan Beach. However after struggling to find a place in the school team, Terry decided to join the Downpatrick Youth Football league where he played for team Santos. Lots of the squads of little boy hopefuls in this league in the county town were exotically named after the best known teams in the world whether they were Irish, British, Brazilian or European. Whilst playing for Santos Terry met Macartan Bryce who was their goalkeeper. They have remained great friends since that time.

Santos was a very successful team where Terry learned his early manoeuvres and scored many goals. Whilst playing for Santos, Terry was spotted by a well known local soccer scout, the late Bill Oakes. Discovering Terry Cochrane must have made Bill's day and it was not long before he was able to set up Terry with an apprenticeship at Nottingham Forest. However this venture did not work out for Terry nor did a similar short term posting at Everton and he soon returned home to Killyleagh. Probably the main reason for his relative early failure was due to homesickness and the difficulty of fitting in at such a young age in a foreign land.

Back at home Terry immediately got the chance to play a few games for the local amateur team, Killyleagh Youth Club. This club, founded in 1960, had been extremely successful from its earliest days, having already won a number of trophies and defeating many sides from the Irish professional divisions.

In 1972, at the age of 19, Terry got his first local opportunity. He was signed by Derry City, the Irish League side which was soon to disappear owing to the trouble and strife emerging in the Maiden City at the beginning of Northern Ireland's 'Troubles'. But for two years until Derry City eventually left the league, Terry gained his initial opportunity in semi-professional football. We must remember that he probably only earned around £5 per week and had to make his way back to county Down after his matches. He recalls once returning to Belfast from the north west only to miss the last bus home. He had to walk all the way home to Killyleagh.

When Derry City closed down Terry was taken on by Linfield, Belfast's premier football club. This was an even better opportunity for Terry and he was in their squad for a short time. One day he met Bertie Peacock, the former Celtic and Northern Ireland player and also the Coleraine manager, at Windsor Park and he suggested to Terry that he should move to Coleraine

Terry shows his skill on the ball against the boys from Killyleagh

where he considered his chances would be better. Terry looks back on this meeting as the turning point in his football career.

Still barely 20 years old, his career was now beginning to blossom. Terry then moved to Coleraine to join the staff of Peacock's up and coming Irish League team. Here he excelled and got his first real opportunities. He played regularly in the first team and scored on many occasions. Terry immediately became a favourite of the Coleraine fans. His name was always appearing in the local newspapers with such headlines as – 'Terry is a topper', 'Talented Terry' and, most pleasing to everyone including himself, 'Cochrane's a bit like George Best – an individualist'.

Whilst at Coleraine he had the opportunity to play European football. Northern Irish clubs each year have the chance to contest European competitions but few rarely proceed beyond the first round. Terry played against such excellent clubs as Eintracht Frankfurt and, although they were heavily defeated by the Germans in both ties (6 goals to 2 at Coleraine), the experience gained stood him in great stead throughout his career. He was rewarded for his excellent play by scoring one of the Coleraine consolation goals. To have been able to compete against such world soccer stars was something he never forgot.

The Irish Cup final in 1975 was between Coleraine and Linfield. It took three games for the winners to emerge. At the third attempt Coleraine defeated their Belfast rivals by one goal to nil. Although Terry was not the scorer he gave, nonetheless, '90 minutes of non-stop action'.

He continued to play for Coleraine and, in September 1975, he was nominated as the 'Player of the Month'. This greatly pleased him but the fans at the Coleraine Showgrounds were even more delighted. His prize was a cheque for £50. At that time he was earning, as a player, the princely sum of £9 per week.

The name of Terry Cochrane was becoming synonymous with every perfect footballing skill and his enthusiasm for the game was clear for all to see. It was now time for the Northern Ireland selectors to sit up and take notice. In due course, after some persistent prodding from football pundits and the crowds at Coleraine, they did. The manager, Dave Clements, decided to include Terry in his Northern Ireland squad to play Norway in the European Cup qualifiers in October 1975. Terry was delighted as were his friends throughout Northern Ireland. Telegrams of congratulation poured in to his home and to Coleraine's headquarters. His chance had come and he had been chosen as an international player whilst still playing for an Irish League Club.

The game against Norway took place at Windsor Park in Belfast. Terry had, of course, played there before for the Linfield side and so he knew what to expect from the crowds. Or at least he thought he did. However he had not reckoned with the vast difference from playing a league game compared with an international one. The atmosphere was entirely different from an ordinary Linfield game and the crowds were much larger. The anticipation of playing for one's country struck home with the young Cochrane. He was nervous. At just 22 he was being given the opportunity he had always dreamed about. In the event he was brought on as a substitute in the second half and experienced first hand the thrill of not only playing in the international colours for the first time but also of being part of a winning team. Northern Ireland beat Norway 3 goals to nil that evening.

Terry's joy at playing for Northern Ireland was summed up in his own words – 'Once you put on the green, you're a man inspired'. However he was to be badly disappointed that the Northern Ireland managers did not pick him again for well over two years. The reasons seem flimsy. He was playing exceedingly well and, according to the soccer journalists, should have been picked again much sooner. But he had to bide his time and wait patiently for his next chance to play in a Northern Ireland jersey which came eventually in May 1978 against Scotland.

2.
Life in the Fast Lane

Terry was now ready to move to an English club. His player manager at Coleraine, Ivan Murray, believed that a call would soon come from 'across the water'. In October 1976 that call came in the guise of Harry Potts, the manager of the English Second Division team, Burnley. Terry admits that he was not even sure where he was going but accepted the offer. He was transferred for the sum of £28,000. Not only was this a terrific boost to Terry himself but the money helped Coleraine out of some financial troubles.

Terry scored in his first two games for his new club. He was an immediate success for the fans and his new player colleagues. To play for the 'Clarets' was a real thrill for Terry and, for Burnley, the arrival of the Northern Irish international proved a life saver. The team had not been prospering in the Second Division and the prospect of relegation was, if not imminent, a distinct possibility.

Once again the local newspapers and the club magazine extolled the virtues of their new signing. They praised his 'twinkling feet'; they acknowledged him 'saving Burnley from ignominious defeat' on occasion; they delighted in his 'brilliant games'. He was regularly acclaimed as the 'Claret Star' – the Burnley magazine's award for the best player of the week. Turf Moor (the Burnley ground) was warming to Terry Cochrane and he was warming to the local fans and players.

Burnley, at that time, had the reputation of being 'the master wheelers and dealers of soccer flesh and blood' – no mean acclamation for any football club. Terry fitted neatly into this type of atmosphere. He enjoyed the game and put everything he had into the Saturday league and cup matches. He scored 17 times in his 75 appearances for the club and the 'Irish ace' was instrumental in Burnley achieving the fine wins the team had over Glasgow Celtic in the 1978 Anglo Scottish Cup. This competition amongst a select number of the best Scottish and English teams took the format of a home and an away tie. On 12 September 1978 Burnley defeated Celtic at home by one goal to nil, a result which clearly did not please the Celtic fans. As a consequence they caused a riot which resulted in a very ugly atmosphere for the Burnley players and their fans. The following week, at Parkhead in Glasgow, Burnley won again, this time by two goals to one. Happily there were no altercations after that match.

But by this time Terry was growing unsettled at Burnley and made it known that he would like a move to another, preferably a First Division, club. Before the year was out the manager of Middlesbrough, John Neal, approached Terry and the Burnley staff and offered Burnley a sum they could not refuse for their Northern Irish international — £210,000. This amount was one of the largest transfer fees in the English League at the time and it was quickly accepted.

The fee also helped Coleraine for, as part of their original agreement with Burnley, they were entitled to receive 25% of the fee if Terry moved to another club within a certain time. This was the case, so the Irish club netted £52,500. On the foot of this huge amount of money – at least for Coleraine it was a massive sum – they built a new stand and other much needed facilities at the club. And so it was that, in effect, Coleraine had Terry Cochrane to thank for the vast improvements at the Showgrounds. They really should have named the new stand 'the Terry Cochrane stand' but they did not. And in any case Terry would not have wished this.

The move to Middlesbrough

With their new record signing, Middlesbrough's manager and fans sat back to see just how good their new player would be. They were not to be disappointed. Terry's maxim – 'When I get the ball, I move forward' – was exactly the right attitude. The Middlesbrough folk liked their new boy and were impressed by his magic performances against the other First Division greats, such as Manchester United and Spurs. Terry remembered the night his old team, Burnley, had defeated those London masters,

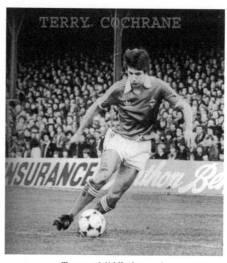

Terry at Middlesborough

Tottenham Hotspur. The larger crowds with the resultant excited cheering and whistling spurred on young Cochrane and his new club seemed more than pleased with him. He scored and always gave his utmost in the weekly encounters against their mighty opponents.

However life at Ayresome Park for 'crafty Cochrane' became a bit frustrating during 1979 when Terry found himself more often than not on the substitutes' bench or in the reserve team. He was finding it difficult to get a first team place. But philosophical as ever Terry put it all down to experience and within a few months he was back in favour and turning out for the firsts more regularly.

Middlesbrough fans, according to Terry, were extremely passionate. They loved their football and appreciated the skills of their players. Terry was tremendously popular and was seen as one of the team's most exciting players. A goal he scored against Swansea is remembered and talked about to this day. It is considered to be one of the two best goals ever scored by a Middlesbrough player. The goal features in a current video of Middlesbrough's 'greatest goals of all time'. Terry was 'on his day that rare thing – a genuine crowd pleaser'. This epitomised Terry's career with the First Division club.

The sight of Terry Cochrane, with his socks down around his ankles showing his shin guard free legs, will be something the Middlesbrough people will not easily forget. By 1983, however, with Malcolm Allison now manager, Terry felt the urge to move. He had never totally gelled with Allison and, rather than having any unseemly bust-up, he sought another club. A free transfer to Third Division club, Gillingham, for the 'willowy, dribbling winger', 'the skilful, but temperamental' Terry Cochrane beckoned. By mid 1983 he had moved to the Kent club with no regrets but with many happy memories at Middlesbrough.

Gillingham Football Club

Terry probably didn't realise it at the time, but his short stay at Third Division Gillingham was to be his happiest time playing in the English League. He moved there at the start of the 1983/4 season on a free transfer and was immediately a hit with the fans. Before long, in fact within a few months, he was even voted the club's most popular player. The club was struggling in the division but still the locals came to see 'the joker in the pack, the skilful crowd pleaser and the big hit with fans and players alike'.

The manager, Keith Peacock, was a fine man and popular with everyone. But, as Terry said, he was on a hiding to nothing. Yet he soldiered on and, with Terry now voted Third Division Player of the Year in 1984, he knew he at least had players who would try their best for the club regardless of its lowly position in the league.

Terry scored a decent number of goals for Gillingham but the one which everyone remembered was against Bristol Rovers. The goalkeeper knocked the ball out to Terry close to the midway line. He turned and chipped the ball 45 yards right into the opposition net over the keeper's head. Their keeper was completely fooled and the crowd went wild. This strike was voted the best goal ever seen at Gillingham. Terry Cochrane could do no wrong. He was their hero.

He was also full of fun on the pitch. He never allowed any situation to get too serious. When taking a corner kick when tempers were getting a bit frayed in the goal mouth, Terry would take a moment's time out to rub his nose on the corner flag. On at least one occasion, feeling that none of his team was bothering to pass the ball to him, he left the field and sat down beside a lady supporter on a vacant seat in the stand. 'If they're not going to pass the ball to me', he said to the mesmerised lady, 'I might as well sit here and watch the game'. The crowd exploded in laughter.

But the best story is when Terry was awarded a throw-in and rushed to get the ball to take a quick advantage. He grabbed the ball and it was only then, as it very slowly slipped out of his hand, that he realised that the 'ball' was in fact a balloon. Players and crowd alike were in paroxysms of laughter. Perhaps they all felt that they might score quicker with the balloon rather than with the ball.

Before leaving the club, by way of a fitting farewell, Terry was acknowledged, by press and fans alike, as 'the most exciting player most of them had ever seen at the club'. With this acclamation ringing in his ears, he went on to make a couple of final appearances for Northern Ireland late in 1983 and early in 1984.

After leaving Gillingham he joined Millwall. But this was only a short stay for, after only four games, Terry picked up an Achilles tendon injury which prevented him from continuing to play.

Terry eventually moved to Hartlepool Football Club in 1985. His period there was even shorter than at Millwall. Injuries affected him yet again and he decided, after just a couple of games there, that he would give up the professional career and return to amateur football. By the age of 32 Terry Cochrane's top flight league football days were over. He had not regretted one moment. He considered that having played his beloved soccer professionally for well over 10 years was reward enough. Pastures new would mean less pressure and more time for his family.

3.
An International Career

Ever since he had been a boy it was Terry's ambition to play international football. To represent his country was a goal he was determined to achieve. The green jersey of Northern Ireland was firstly a dream but then, as he started to play professional football, his clear objective. He was to discover, however, that playing for one's country was an up and down business.

In October 1975, whilst playing for Coleraine, Terry received his first call up from the then manager of Northern Ireland, Dave Clements. For weeks beforehand the press was howling at Clements to include 'Coleraine's wing wizard' in the squad for the European Cup qualifiers. Clements relented and called up Terry for the match against Norway in Belfast on 29 October 1975.

The excitement for Terry and his friends and family, not to mention his Coleraine colleagues, was almost unbearable. Telegrams came in from all parts wishing the Killyleagh lad the best of luck in his first call up and fervently hoping that he would actually play in the game. Come the night of the encounter, Terry started on the substitutes' bench. Northern Ireland were in sparkling form and were winning the game easily when Clements sent Terry on with around 20 minutes to go. He played impressively and unquestionably enhanced the performance of a rampant Northern Ireland team. The final score was 3-0. It was an excellent start to the team's forthcoming campaign.

But then, as often is the case, the Northern Ireland management, soon to be under the legendary Danny Blanchflower, promptly forgot Terry Cochrane. Try as he might to catch their eye in subsequent league and cup matches, it was another two and a half years before he once again donned that coveted green strip. By this time, of course, Terry had moved to Burnley and, although he was playing his usual inventive football there, he must have thought that his chances of further football for Northern Ireland were remote.

However all good things came to those who waited. For Terry it was the 1978 Home Championship competition which was to resurrect his international career. In those days the four home nations, England, Wales, Scotland and Northern Ireland, played against each other for the honour of winning the Home Nations Championship. Northern Ireland rarely won the prize but they had done so in this era. Terry got his chance against all three opponents in May 1978 but always as substitute. The best result Northern Ireland achieved that year was a draw against Scotland and defeats to England and Wales. However Terry acquitted himself well but must have wondered if he would ever get a full game.

Later that year in the European World Cup qualifiers Northern Ireland were drawn against Denmark, Bulgaria, the Republic of Ireland and their 'bete noire', England. Terry was chosen for five of these preliminary matches which were played between September 1978 and May 1979. In four of the games he played the entire 90 minutes and was again substitute in Dublin against the Republic. Although he did not score Terry was considered one of the team's best and most imaginative players. Of these five games Northern Ireland were twice winners over Bulgaria, once over Denmark, earned a draw with the Republic and lost to England. Those were the good days for Northern Ireland football.

Terry scores an international goal

In March 1980 Northern Ireland played a disappointing draw against Israel in Tel Aviv. Terry played but, like his team mates, he only just about managed to acquit himself tolerably well. However when the Home Championships took place once more in May, Terry was to find the back of the net.

Against, of all teams, England Terry scored his first international goal at Wembley Stadium in London on 20 May, one of the very few Northern Ireland players to have achieved this distinction. The Northern Ireland fans who had travelled to the capital more in hope than in expectation were ecstatic. To score an international goal was something for any local player to celebrate but to score one against England was just about the absolute pinnacle of their career. Very few goals have been scored by Northern Ireland against England but here was Terry Cochrane taking his place amongst such 'greats' as Terry Neill, George Best and, of course, David Healy. This particular game ended in a 1-1 draw.

As it should happen, I was in the crowd at Wembley in 1972 when Terry Neill's goal was enough to defeat the English team. I remember the silence and disbelief of the England fans and the excitement of the handful of Northern Ireland supporters who there present that evening.

Three days later Terry played against Wales and his side proved victorious by one goal to nil. Terry did not play against Scotland but Northern Ireland won the championship that year – and Terry had contributed magnificently to their success.

By now Terry, of course, was a Middlesbrough player and 20 of his international caps were won when he was playing for them.

In the summer of 1980 the Northern Ireland team went on a tour of Australia where matches were played in Sydney, Melbourne, Adelaide and Perth. Terry played in all four games and scored twice in a 4-0 win in Perth. As Murphy's or Sod's law would have it, however, this particular game was not deemed an international but simply a friendly. Therefore Terry was deprived of an additional two international goals because of some administrative hiccup. The other three matches in Australia were full internationals where Terry played his heart out but did not manage to score. As ever he was pleased to have done well and entertained the crowds, although he did feel a little 'hard done by' at not having the two goals at Perth added to his international tally.

The 1982 World Cup campaign

With the World Cup scheduled to take place in Spain in 1982, Northern Ireland was anxious to do well. At that time they had an exceptional squad and Terry Cochrane was firmly amongst those hoping to play in the world's premier football tournament. As ever the preliminary rounds or qualifiers commenced over a year and a half before the event. Northern Ireland had been drawn with Scotland, Sweden and Portugal – a fairly formidable trio of talented teams.

Terry was destined to play in five of these matches which started off with an encounter against Sweden in Belfast. In this game Terry came on as a substitute and Northern Ireland won 3-0 at Windsor Park. A month later, however, they lost 1-0 to Portugal in Lisbon and a 1-1 draw with Scotland in March 1981 left Northern Ireland's chances of qualifying in the balance.

A win over Portugal, unlikely as it might have seemed, was the only result which would keep them in contention. The match in Belfast was a tight tussle but, by well into the second half, there was still no score. Things were soon to change, however, when Terry's 'dancing and dribbling' skills helped to break the deadlock. He ran down the wing beating off the Portuguese challenges and chipped a supremely accurate pass over to Gerry Armstrong who weaved around the fullbacks and slotted the ball into the net. Northern Ireland had won this crucial tie and seemed almost certain to qualify.

In Sweden in June, however, the result went against Northern Ireland when they lost 1-0 but, in the end, they were to qualify for the World Cup finals for the first time since 1958 in Sweden. Joy was unbounded for everyone especially Terry Cochrane. His next greatest ambition was about to be fulfilled — firstly to play for Northern Ireland and then to be a member of their World Cup squad.

It seemed virtually certain that Terry would be picked. He had, after all, played in five of the qualifying matches and had acquitted himself well. His inch perfect pass to Armstrong that night against Portugal had well nigh copper fastened Northern Ireland's qualification. But fate was once again to intervene.

Terry picked up a hamstring injury during a friendly match against France in March 1982 at the Parc des Princes in Paris. Try as he might he could not throw off the injury and it continued to niggle him for weeks. He knew he had to come clean with the Northern Ireland manager, Billy Bingham, and declare his injury. Everything was done to help Terry recover but to no avail. He could not be included in the squad for Spain. Most people would have been absolutely devastated but Terry was philosophical. It was just one of those things and injuries like his could have affected any one of his colleagues.

Northern Ireland's success in Spain during that campaign has been well documented. Their 1-0 win over the host nation at Valencia after Gerry Armstrong's brilliant goal, as well as Pat Jennings' inspired and brave goalkeeping after Mal Donaghy had been sent off leaving Northern Ireland with just ten men, is the stuff of local legend. Although they did not progress beyond the quarter finals in the competition they had covered themselves with glory and they were hailed as heroes upon their return to Belfast.

Terry Cochrane could only watch the television screen to follow his team's fortunes. Had he been luckier and escaped injury he could well have contributed to Northern Ireland's run of success. It was not to be, but he was proud of all that his colleagues had done. It is comforting to note that Billy Bingham was so disappointed that Terry had not been able to travel that he arranged for him to receive exactly the same fees as his playing team mates had earned whilst in Spain. Such was Bingham's affection for, and trust in, his little Killyleagh winger.

Terry's international career was by now slowly winding down. After his 24th cap against France in March 1982 when he was injured, Terry felt that his days for playing for Northern Ireland were at an end. However, after he had moved to Gillingham, he was recalled to play against Scotland in Belfast in December 1983. Northern Ireland won the match by two goals to nil and Terry had played for the entire game. It always felt good to record a win against the old adversary, especially when Terry had not played for his country for some time.

But the end was near and Terry's appearance as a substitute against Finland away from home in the World Cup qualifying match in May 1984, which Northern Ireland lost 1-0 (although once again they qualified for the 1986 World Cup), was to be his swansong. At the age of 31 Terry Cochrane had completed his international career. He had played in 26 internationals and, although only scoring one goal, it had notably been against their arch rivals, England, at Wembley.

Terry is proud to have played so many times for Northern Ireland and he will be long remembered as being one of the chosen few who scored against England. Nothing could ever take that distinction away from him.

4.
Football Abroad

Many professional footballers as they reach the end of their domestic careers take the opportunity – if one arises – to play abroad, often in countries where association football is not the leading sport. And so it was for Terry Cochrane.

His first opportunity came during his period as a Middlesbrough player. A window of opportunity opened when he was asked to go to Hong Kong late in 1982, and for nine months he played in the local professional league with the Eastern team. There Bobby Moore was the playing coach and Trevor Brooking was one of his team mates. Terry got to know these legendary English internationals very well and has retained their friendship in later years.

Football in Hong Kong was little less than a frenetic activity for all the teams in the league. All teams played at the one magnificent stadium on Hong Kong Island. Most of the teams in the league had a number of foreign players in the squad alongside the local talent. In the Eastern side with Terry and Bobby as coach were other ex-Northern Ireland internationals, including Derek Spence. The Seiko team had lots of Dutch players; the Chin Wans had Brazilians and Eastern with the English and Northern Irish.

Crowds at these games were large and enthusiastic and Terry remembered that at his games there were often as many as 10,000 spectators. He scored on eight occasions for the team and he said that the cheers were every bit as passionate as they had been when he was playing for Northern Ireland. When the local lads and their Brazilian team mates played there could have been as many as 25,000 roaring and adoring fans. Football in Hong Kong, in those days before China regained control of the colony, was the biggest and most popular sport. The foreign players, like Terry, greatly enhanced the game and their skills and professional bearing contributed much to give real enjoyment to the people of Hong Kong.

In his spare time, whenever he had any, Terry – whose wife and two sons had not been able to join him – explored the rich culture of both the island and the mainland. The famous Star ferries frantically plying across Hong Kong harbour gave him immense pleasure when he left his hotel off Nathan Road to visit some of the beautiful villages on Hong Kong Island. Although he never visited China, which would have been almost impossible anyway, he did enjoy the wonderful sights of the ancient temples and picturesque gardens which proliferate on the mainland part of the colony.

Terry returned to England having thoroughly benefited from his Asian experience. To have been able to mix with other former internationals from many countries as well as assisting the local footballers to improve their skills had been a memory he would never forget.

Terry's days at Middlesbrough were over, as he was soon to discover. He moved then, on a free transfer, to Gillingham. These were happy days for him and, by 1985, Terry began seriously to think about his future in the beautiful game.

The Dallas Sidekicks

But before he finally had to make up his mind, a further international opportunity turned up. Lots of slightly older professional players in the British Isles were being invited to play in the United States where soccer was beginning to take hold. Terry was pleased to be offered a short contract with a Dallas team called the Sidekicks and he left home in England, this time with Etta, his wife, and Paul and Steven, his sons, for Texas.

Terry's offer to join the Sidekicks came from Gordon Jago who, as a Charlton player in the 1950s and a manager for Millwall and Queen's Park Rangers, was well respected on the world soccer scene. Terry got to know and to value Gordon's enthusiasm and experience whilst in America.

This was to be yet another experience Terry would never forget. This time, however, it was not to turn out to be so enjoyable. The people were friendly, but the football was different, to say the least. Terry had never before played league football indoors. The Sidekicks' home was in a large stadium which doubled up as a basketball arena. The game itself was not exactly 'regulation'. Although there were eleven players on each team, they played in rotation with only seven or so on the 'field' at any one time. Terry found it hard to explain but it was not really to his liking. Of course, he played skilfully for his team, to the best of his ability in the unusual circumstances, but it was not for him. The local crowds, however, like in all American sports, were absolutely crazy about their team and followed them through thick and thin

Terry remained in Texas for just five months. He visited other famous American cities such as Wichita and Memphis when he was playing away matches for the Sidekicks and even passed close to, but unfortunately had not the time to visit, Elvis Presley's Graceland home. Terry put the American footballing interlude down to experience.

On his return to England he was to complete his brief stay with Millwall (where he played with the England international, Teddy Sheringham) and Hartlepool and, by 1986, his professional career was over – hamstring and Achilles tendon injuries saw to that. He then joined the ranks of amateur football which he was to greatly enjoy.

Want to be a coach in Saudi Arabia?

Early in 1991 Terry was reading the daily newspaper – it happened to be the *Daily Mirror* – when he read an advertisement which interested him. At this time he was 38 years old and was playing amateur football in his local area. The advertisement was seeking football coaches for the Saudi Arabian military. The job appealed to Terry so he quickly got in touch with the prospective employers. They were interviewing in London and, when Terry arrived, he was almost immediately offered the position.

There were going to be pros and cons if he accepted the post. He would not be able to take his family to the Middle Eastern Kingdom and he would be away from home for most of a year. Having discussed the situation with his wife, he decided to accept and soon found himself in the sands of Arabia. He was posted to the ancient city of Jedda where he was to train the Saudi military team. The lads were good enough footballers and were keen to learn their game from the former Northern Ireland star.

The only problem for Terry was that, when he was there, the Gulf War was raging and the soldiers were often ordered off to the front on the borders of the invaded Kuwait. This meant that there were no trainees on many occasions leaving Terry with time on his hands. This was, of course, no real hardship in such a country as Saudi Arabia. At the fabulous stadium where the training took place, which incidentally held 30,000 spectators, there was also an Olympic size swimming pool and all sorts of fitness suites. Terry simply made use of these wonderful facilities, kept fit and waited for the return of his young charges.

He made many friends there one of whom was the King's chief helicopter pilot who, from time to time, had to leave at the drop of a hat to attend to his Sovereign's wishes.

In such a wealthy country there were countless receptions for the foreigners who stayed in the compound set aside for the likes of Terry and his colleagues. There were a number of occasions when he met members of the Royal Family and he even saw King Fahd at one of these levees. This was an entirely different world from living in English suburbia but was an experience which Terry would never have missed.

There was not any opportunity to visit any other Saudi cities but Terry found the city of Jedda entirely fabulous and exciting. To have spent this period of his life in such a rarefied atmosphere was yet another 'never to be forgotten' episode and he also had the satisfaction of having improved the skills of young Saudi soccer stars of the future. Many did, in fact, play for the Saudi Arabian team in international matches in the years to come.

Spending nearly a year in the heat of the desert without his family was a lonely experience and Terry was glad to return home. He knew, however, that he had made a success of his stay in Saudi Arabia and there were many young Saudi internationals who could thank Northern Ireland's Terry Cochrane for teaching them the skills and ability required for the great game. Perhaps, like Terry, they had learned the thrill of going forward with the ball rather than on the emphasis of just passing it around. They would have agreed with Terry's well known, but not always appreciated, maxim – 'when you get the ball, go forward'.

5.
Is There Life Beyond Professional Football?

Terry saw the move to amateur football as the natural progression for his game. He had enjoyed playing in front of large and boisterous crowds over many years at club and international level. He had savoured the exotic game, so to speak, in America, Hong Kong and Saudi Arabia. Now it was time to hang up the professional boots and see what the amateur game could offer.

He looked forward to this new pace of football. In 1987, after his short stay at Hartlepool, Terry joined the elegantly named Billingham Synthonia, or the 'Synners' as they were nicknamed. For four years he played week by week in front of small crowds of enthusiastic people who enjoyed watching the amateur teams in the Northern League. Billingham, with Terry as an essential member of the team, made a great deal of progress in those four years. They won the 2nd division title and were immediately crowned as the 1st division champions. In 1989, Terry was to win his only English cup as a member of the Billingham squad. These were enjoyable footballing days for a star who was in his late thirties.

When Terry left the 'Synners' in 1989 he became, for the first time, a manager of a football team. For a relatively short period of some months during 1992 and 1993, Terry played for, and managed, two other Northern League clubs, South Bank and Ferryhill. Both these teams came from the Middlesbrough area. Unfortunately both clubs lacked sufficient finance to keep going and both sadly fell by the wayside. However it had been yet another useful experience for Terry.

Terry's friend and one-time Middlesbrough manager, Steve Gibson, then offered another opportunity to Terry by inviting him to play for his own amateur team, Bulkhaul. This was the name of Steve's company and they regularly played games on Sundays in the North East of England. Terry really loved turning out for this team and enjoyed it even more when they went off each year for a week on a foreign 'tour'. Terry travelled to Germany with the side and as many as six times to Cyprus. It was a more leisurely brand of soccer for the older player – light training and unhurried football with time to relax on the beach or by the pool.

Thus Terry Cochrane arrived at an elegant conclusion to his football career. Apart from the occasional charity match, he no longer plays the game but is now giving back to the community the skills he learnt himself as a boy in Killyleagh and Downpatrick.

Coaching and broadcasting

For some years now Terry, who is the holder of a coveted UEFA 'A' licence, has been coaching youngsters, boys and girls, as part of the Middlesbrough 'Football in the Community' programme. He daily undertakes sessions at the local clubs and in the schools in the town and the surrounding area. He is also taking part in camps for young footballers in Great Britain and Ireland. The former 'will-o'-the-wisp inside forward' from Northern Ireland is contributing to future generations of professional footballers. He would have it no other way – Bill Oakes taught him all he knew; Terry Cochrane will teach the Middlesbrough youngsters all he knows.

Every Saturday Terry now commentates on local Teesside radio on matches involving teams like Hartlepool and Darlington. This appeals greatly to Terry who can now describe the game he played and enjoyed for so long to many eager fans who are unable to get out to the games. His style represents the man he is – informative, intelligent and full of fun. The game comes to life with Terry at the microphone. He is popular with the broadcasters and listeners alike. It may well be that this is Terry's real future in the game.

Terry and the footballing greats

For many years when Terry was playing professional and international football, he was well acquainted with those other great names in the game. When asked how well he knew George Best, Terry would say that he knew him reasonably well. Both men were in the Northern Ireland squad at the end of George's career and the beginning of Terry's. He remained on the substitutes' bench while George played his last game for his country. They got on well together and Terry treasures those brief encounters with that great footballing legend. He will remind people that George did buy him a drink at the Northern Ireland headquarters at the Chimney Corner Hotel outside Belfast. And better still, Terry once played a testimonial match for Jim Platt on the same team as George Best back in the early 1980s.

Other Northern Ireland internationals like Sammy McIlroy, David McCreery, Norman Whiteside, Pat Jennings, Gerry Armstrong, Derek Spence and Martin O'Neill are considered by Terry to be good friends. They played on the same Northern Ireland side and were close to him at that time. Some of them keep in touch from time to time.

Sir Trevor Brooking, formerly of England and now Director of Football Development at the English Football Association, was a member of the same team as Terry in Hong Kong. Steve Bruce, currently manager at Birmingham City was at Gillingham in Terry's days. Steve Kindon who played at Burnley with Terry is another friend. Terry's younger son was even called after him. Steve nowadays is an after dinner speaker of note.

And what of the future?

Many people would have thought that the natural progression for Terry after playing the game would have been to take up a management role somewhere. Many would wonder why he did not become manager of some of the English League clubs. The truth is that he never had a real interest in taking on all these onerous responsibilities. He has, however, admitted that if someone had asked him he might have considered it. But the fact is that, apart from short spells with amateur clubs, no one

Terry depicted on the Killyleagh mural

did approach him. He is philosophical about it – management was not coming his way. Coaching was and is his forte. He thinks that his work in this field is worthwhile and satisfying. He may not be in the limelight but he knows that he is encouraging many young people to play the game. This is reward itself.

Terry has had the support of his wife, Etta, and his two sons, Paul and Steven, throughout his career. They have lived in Middlesbrough for a long time and have made many friends there. Paul is now married and has a little son, Thomas. Steven has left home but lives very close to his parents. Contacts with family in Northern Ireland remain important and as many visits as are possible are made there each year. He always makes a point of catching up with his friend, Macartan Bryce and his wife, Geraldine, who introduced Terry to his wife, Etta, in the early days.

Terry has no regrets. From his days playing for youth clubs and the Scouts to his days with professional clubs, to his days abroad and with amateur teams have gone to make up the rich tapestry of the football career of Terry Cochrane.

As a son of modern day Killyleagh Terry Cochrane can be assured of a place in the village's hall of fame. His likeness now adorns the 'Killyleagh International Football Legends' mural off Frederick Street along with those of Hugh Henry Davey and David Healy. Killyleagh has been fortunate to have Terry as a famous son. The young man who was described as being 'head and shoulders above the 21 others on the field' and one whom 'we will not see his like again' continues to contribute to the next generation of amateur and professional footballers.

David Healy

1.
Football as an Early Way of Life

'David is a good all-rounder. He works well in class and enjoys PE and games a lot – a future footballer, I'm quite sure!' These words of Miss Zena McAllister, who was David's first teacher at Killyleagh Primary School, turned out to be truly prophetic. At the early age of five, David's supreme talent had already been spotted, not by a professional team scout, but by a perceptive school teacher.

Born on Sunday 5 August 1979, David Jonathan Healy was the youngest of Clifford and Irene Healy's three children. Their older son, Clifford, had been born in 1978 and their daughter, Lana, in 1975. Their home was in the sleepy village of Killyleagh, the home of so many remarkable people over the centuries.

When David was enrolled at the 'White' school, the Primary School below the impressive castle, he was already more than just a budding footballer. He was a determined little boy who knew what he wanted to be – even in those early days. According to his mother, David slept with a football in his bed from a very early age. When he rose in the morning his first thoughts and actions revolved round football. He was outside the house kicking the ball against the wall unless he had been able to persuade his father or brother – or any unsuspecting neighbour – to join in. There was no doubt that, before long, David would want to be a member of a real football team.

Two early opportunities came by the age of six or seven. At Primary school there was, naturally enough, a football team. No self respecting Northern Irish school was without one. In primary four, when he was seven, David pestered the teacher to let him play in the team, which normally consisted of boys from primary six and seven. The teacher had to be pragmatic. He wanted his team to do well and he knew the prodigious talent of young Healy, regardless of his age. There was no argument. David Healy would play and when he showed that he could score goals and weave around his much taller opponents the Killyleagh team went from strength to strength. They won everything before them.

David, even from such a young age however, was never totally immersed in football. Throughout his life he participated in every club or organisation which would give him experiences – and, if football was included, so much the better. He joined the Killyleagh Parish Scout Group's Beaver colony in 1985 and, when the chance arose, was showing his pals the way to play, and enjoy, football.

But this part time football was not enough for the feisty little seven year old. There had to be football leagues where he could play against all sorts of other teams from the area. Wearing the football boots and donning the team jersey was his sole ambition. The opportunity soon came. His father, Clifford, no mean footballer himself for the local Killyleagh Youth Club team, encouraged his son to go to join the local under 12 Killyleagh team which was in the Downpatrick league.

The team's manager, David Brown, knew the Healys well and certainly had been impressed by young David Healy. So it was that David became a member of the team. He kitted out every Saturday morning but had to stand on the sidelines for most of the match until his manager, fully realising his talent but concerned at the lad's diminutive size, allowed him to play for the last ten minutes of the game. Not only did the little maestro play his heart out, but he even had the audacity to score goals. He was an instant success – but still only seven and just four feet tall.

Moving up a league

When David was ten years old he left the Killyleagh team and joined the team in Crossgar just a few miles from home. There the team was a member of two District Youth Leagues – in Downpatrick and in Ballynahinch. His managers there, Tom Skeffington and Paul Taggart, often had the problem of not knowing which game David should play in. If it was possible at all, and the kick-off times suited, then David played in both league matches on a Saturday. He was rushed from one venue to another and invariably scored in both matches.

With the Crossgar team David won the District Knock Out Cup in 1989. He won a number of other trophies and was named 'Best Player of the Year'. 'The scourge of so many teams', he scored 40 goals in the under 12 league. He scored regular hat-tricks and his 'golden goals' meant that he was almost always the side's top scorer. The local newspapers were filled week after week with photographs of the winning Crossgar teams, with David Healy prominently positioned in the front row. Aged ten, he was already a personality but, modest as ever, he thought little of the publicity and concentrated on what he did best – scoring goals.

Although he had left his first Killyleagh club, David was still able to squeeze in Saturday afternoon games back in Killyleagh. There he joined the Killyleagh Tigers helping them to win league and cup doubles. His Primary School team played in the Mid Down Schools League and as David continued to score and his team went on winning, they succeeded in being crowned Champions in 1991, David's last year in Primary School.

Not just satisfied with playing in Crossgar and Killyleagh on a Saturday, and with his school during the week, he also played for the local Boys' Brigade team. When an opportunity arose to play football David Healy was ready and willing.

Lisburn Youth Football Club

Even before David had left Primary School and still aged ten, he was recruited for the even more prestigious Lisburn Youth team. He played for their various teams, off and on, for the next six years. As he was weaned away from the Crossgar team, he immediately proved his flair with his new team's under 11s, scoring six times in an early game against Glengormley. When he was in the under 13s team he hit the back of the net ten times against an unfortunate team called Blue Star. He helped the team win the Northern Ireland Championship.

The smiling face or the shots at goal of young David were now regularly featured, not only in the local Downpatrick papers, but now in the Lisburn and even the Belfast ones. It was by now something unusual not to have a picture of the little Killyleagh star in the weekly papers. 'Deadly David' and 'the ace marksman David Healy' were just a couple of the punchy headlines attributed to the rising football star.

In a period of just four years at Lisburn David scored an incredible 350 goals. One year he scored 126 times and the next

107 – these achievements remain a club record to this day. It was perfectly normal to see him score two hat-tricks or even more in one game. His team was simply demolishing their opposition sometimes winning by a margin of 17-0. With David Healy on board it seemed that no team could lose. They did, of course, occasionally succumb to defeat but very seldom.

Playing in the League at Lisburn, under manager Les King, also offered further exciting opportunities for David. In the summer of 1995, the team received an invitation to go to southern California to compete in the annual Surf Cup competition in San Diego. Over a period of three action filled weeks, Lisburn Youth team played many matches and, in the competition itself, proved unstoppable. In the preliminary rounds they topped their league and then progressed with ruthless precision through the quarter and semi finals to meet a team from England, Salford Boys, in the final. Although the English lads scored first, Lisburn went on to win comfortably 4-2. They had shown 'remarkable skill and fighting spirit to overcome tough opposition from various teams from the States'.

The most notable achievement of the entire tournament was that David Healy scored in every match and it was not at all surprising that he was voted as the 'Most Valuable Player' of the competition. The entire trip had been an unprecedented success and invitations were received by the team to play in all sorts of forthcoming events. The boys arrived home proud of their outstanding triumph and they were hailed as footballing heroes in both the local and the Northern Ireland press. A number of the lads also returned sporting blond hairstyles – a memory of the United States that stayed with them until their next visit to their barbers.

Probably the most remarkable aspect of David's early career in football was the fact that he was part of so many football teams. When not playing for Lisburn or as a Northern Ireland representative, he was able to join the local Killyleagh side under Dee Heron. The manager got word that David was available, often at very short notice, and promptly picked him for the team. He contributed to Killyleagh's fine run of success in those years of the middle to late 1990s and, although he only played around six or seven games for the club, he was always a valued player. He scored his first goal for Killyleagh when he was just 16 years old.

An important feature of David's early career was his popularity and there were never any complaints when he just appeared in the team. Someone had lost his place for the day but the chance to have David in the team almost always ensured its success. He was ever modest, reminding everyone that he was simply part of a team, not the mainstay – although to many he was just that.

2.
A Career with Manchester United

A great friend of the Healy family is Maurice Garrett. He and Clifford Healy have always given stalwart service to the football club at Killyleagh. Maurice has known David since his earliest days and was probably the first person to fully realise the boy's potential. When David was only nine years old, Maurice approached the local Manchester United scout, Eddie Coulter, whom he knew, and told him about David Healy. He suggested that Coulter, who had spotted and recruited many Northern Ireland boys for the English football giants over the years, should have a look at the lad from Killyleagh.

Before long David was invited to attend the Manchester United School of Excellence which, in Belfast, was held at the Olympia Leisure Centre on the Boucher Road. This meant a regular and weekly commitment to training and showing his footballing skills. David went up to Belfast every week for years and was often watched at training and at practice matches by the Manchester United manager, Sir Alex Ferguson. David impressed those watching him who included not only the manager but also stars of the game like Nobby Stiles and Brian Robson. David was now rubbing shoulders with the football greats and it was clearly his intention not only to impress them but also to make sure he got his opportunity to play for this most prestigious team.

In January 1994 his chance came and he signed schoolboy forms for the great Manchester United. There

David with Sir Alex Ferguson

David meeting Sir Bobby Charlton (left) and Sir Matt Busby

was, however, almost a hiccup. Not long before Eddie Coulter got David to sign up, Glasgow Rangers invited him to go to Scotland for a few days and play a few matches for them. It looked as if Rangers might steal a march on Manchester United and beat them to the signature. With one of his football heroes, Ally McCoist of Rangers looking on, David scored a couple of goals for the Glasgow team in two youth games for the club. Whilst they were seriously considering their position, Manchester United quickly stepped in and got the signature they wanted.

David was now on the staff of Manchester United, albeit just as a schoolboy recruit. He was, of course, still at school at Down Academy in Downpatrick which meant he had to travel over to Manchester at the weekends. He also managed to squeeze in a Saturday match for Lisburn before flying across to England. He trained over there and played a game for Manchester United Youth and then had to fly back on the Sunday evening to be in time for school on Monday. It was a hectic schedule for such a young boy but one which he relished.

David made steady progress in all the various teams at Manchester United. In the early days he played for their B team to which early schoolboy signings like David aspired. He scored regularly for this team and never had any problems finding his place. He was just 17 years old. The local Manchester United newspaper, *United Review*, featured David often and he won the coveted 'Top of the Class' award on a regular basis. In his first season with this set-up he scored 25 times and helped them win the Lancashire League, Division Two.

By 1998 he was promoted to the A team and was equally successful with them, scoring and exhibiting his ever improving footballing skills. He was one of the club's natural goal scorers. He got the ball, saw the goal and sank it into the back of the net. By now comparisons were being made between himself and the legendary George Best. In fact George had called David 'a special talent' – an accolade of some distinction.

By this stage David was, of course, now living in Manchester which did have its disadvantages as well as its clear advantages. Rather like George Best, David struggled with homesickness when he first arrived in England. Although he did have a wonderful landlady, Brenda, he still yearned for Killyleagh and the people he loved and missed. But he stuck it out through the guidance and support of a combination of Clifford and Irene, his parents, and the paternal help freely given by the Manchester United staff. They all clearly understood David's dilemma. They had often before seen the predicament of Northern Ireland boys coming to live in England. They all realised David's mammoth potential to the club and were determined to see it fulfilled with some judicious tender loving care. They succeeded and David overcame his gremlins. He started enjoying both his football and his new surroundings.

In due course David signed a two year apprenticeship form for the club and, on 1 August 1999, just before his twentieth birthday, signed a four year professional contract. The world now seemed his oyster. However everything did not work out just as he had hoped and planned.

By this time David was having regular games with the reserves. He was not on the team every week but was still a full squad member. Having been on the books of Manchester United for some years, now seemed the opportune time to be breaking into the first team. Ferguson, the manager, had a plethora of skilled players and prolific goal scorers, many of them signed from overseas. It was going to be difficult for Killyleagh's boy wonder to force his way into the top flight team but he did finally make his debut for the first team in the Worthington Cup against Aston Villa in October.

In 1999 he was also chosen for the squad to travel to Omagh in county Tyrone, for a testimonial match following the 1998 bomb outrage in the town. The locals revelled in the atmosphere of such a great club visiting their little ground at St Julian's Road. The visitors overwhelmed Omagh Town 9-0 but the fact that this great club had taken time off from their busy schedule to play in aid of the Omagh Fund was all that mattered. For the discerning Northern Ireland footballing public it was noted, with some pride and satisfaction, that David Healy had been brought on as a substitute. He sparkled for the last minutes of the game which pleased the Omagh fans.

By late 1999, some months after signing his professional contract, David still could not get a regular place in the first team. The newspapers were full of the story that this creative player and regular goal scorer was yet to be chosen for the squad. His career, after seven years on the club's books, seemed to be hitting the rocks. Sitting on the substitutes' bench occasionally and playing for the reserves was not what David Healy, who had spent all these years in Manchester, wanted. Crisis talks took place with Alex Ferguson. He did not need to be reminded that young Healy was already scoring goals internationally for Northern Ireland and yet could never find a place in his first team. Something had to be done.

David asked for a move – or at least a chance to play with another club. Arrangements were made with Port Vale and David moved there on loan in February 2000. He remained there for the next two and a half months. He was immediately selected for their first team and began scoring and enjoying his game again. He thoroughly relished the opportunity to play with older professional players and to work with the friendly staff at the club. The manager, Brian Horton, had given David the chance to gain valuable experience and he will always be thankful to Brian for looking after him so well. It was unfortunate, however, that David's contribution to the team did not save them from relegation that season.

When he returned to Manchester, however, things were as bad as ever and, apart from occasional reserve appearances and once on the field as substitute for Ryan Giggs against Ipswich in December, David's frustration was only too obvious for all to see.

A further loan was arranged with Preston North End and this immediately turned into a full blooded transfer a few days into the new year, 2001. The transfer fee was a cool £1.5 million, the highest amount ever paid out by the club. David moved there with mixed emotions. His beloved Manchester United could not find a place for him so, to ensure that he continued his chances of playing the professional game, the move to Preston was the fillip he needed. His parting shot epitomised his frame of mind. 'Leaving the greatest club in the world may be the best thing I've ever done'. He would now find a regular first team spot playing for the Second Division team. Manchester United's loss was Preston North End's gain.

3.
The International Scene

From his earliest days at the sport of football it seemed clear for all to see that some day David Healy would become a Northern Ireland international. All his life he had supported them although the team had fallen out of the world top 100 footballing nations. The halcyon days for Northern Ireland football at the World Cup in Spain in 1982 and then in Mexico in 1986 had long since passed. They had become nothing more than a journeyman side. Not only were they not winning but they were also failing to score. In due course of time it was David Healy himself who scored the goal which ended the drought of 1,298 minutes for goalless Northern Ireland.

But we must go back in time to discover David's earlier international days. He played first of all for the under 15 Northern Ireland schools team. He had a memorable match in 1995 against the Republic of Ireland in Dublin when he scored two goals resulting in victory for Northern Ireland. This game was at the start of a busy schedule of matches against foreign and home opposition in the first half of 1995. Apart from the match against the Republic there were games against the home countries which Northern Ireland lost but also one in Limavady when they beat Switzerland 2-0 and David was again on the score sheet.

During the Easter break the Northern Ireland team travelled to Graz in Austria where eight sides competed in a tournament. They played creditably well and gave David yet more European experience. He still had not reached his 16th birthday and he had already played football in a number of countries on the continent of Europe. He went on to play for the under 16s and then the under 18s. A place for David in a Northern Ireland squad at any age had become a foregone conclusion.

During the annual Milk Cup competition at Coleraine the Northern Ireland under 19 side conquered the best from home and abroad. They defeated Feyenoord from the Netherlands in the final and, in this match, David scored a hat-trick. Again he was the pick of the players on show during this week of soccer frenzy in the county Londonderry town.

Playing under 19 international games David continued in his outstanding fashion. In August 1999 he helped Northern Ireland defeat France 3-1 although, in the same event, they lost to Turkey and Finland. But a 1-0 win over the giants of Europe, Germany, helped restore their confidence and boost their morale once more.

Life may have been uncertain at Manchester United but a different opening was soon to lighten the gloom for David. An international career at senior level was beckoning. His chance came early in 2000.

A full international

The football press throughout England and Northern Ireland were full of two aspects of David Healy's career in those early days of the new millennium. Would he ever get a start in the first team at Manchester United where he had spent so many years and would he soon be capped for Northern Ireland?

The first matter was resolved when it became obvious that he probably would not get a full-time place on the first team at Manchester United and so he was sent on loan to Port Vale in February 2000. There he would, at least, become a first team player.

The second issue was, in many ways, more quickly determined. Sammy McElroy, the relatively new manager of Northern Ireland, was known to favour picking young Healy for his squad and he decided that the upcoming match on 23 February 2000 would be the debut for the Killyleagh lad. The team travelled to Luxembourg where they took on another of Europe's footballing minnows. The star of the game, and the scorer of two of the three goals, was David Healy. The words of one of the reporters at the time summed up the highlights of his inspired debut.

'What a debut for the young striker. He scored twice and created another...international football looks as though it was made for Healy'. The local Downpatrick papers were just as ecstatic – David had become 'the Northern Ireland sensation; the Killyleagh kid who had become an international star'. With these acclamations ringing in his ears, David felt he now could look forward to a glittering career in the Northern Ireland team.

David's international career did, in fact, take off. For the next five years right until the present day, he has rarely been overlooked by any of the Northern Ireland managers. A place in the side for David Healy was almost a given. After his outstanding debut against Luxembourg he played three more games in 2000 and scored in two of these games. He found the net in the game in Malta and then scored the team's consolation goal against Yugoslavia. To have scored in three of his first four international games was almost unheard of in terms of the Northern Ireland side.

A serious lack of goals for the Northern Ireland team

The year 2002 started off relatively well for Northern Ireland. In their first four games against Denmark, Iceland, Malta and Poland, they notched up two wins, gained one draw and succumbed to just one defeat. David scored in two of the games, including one against Denmark when he powered the ball past the world renowned goalkeeper, Peter Schmeichel. This was one of David's favourite goals. His international goal tally was now eight and the record number of international goals for Northern Ireland was just thirteen. In a short time, therefore, David's excellent progress seemed sure to attain the record of fourteen.

However the situation drastically changed when they were not able to score against probably the smallest footballing nation, Liechtenstein. That goalless draw did not augur well for the side and, for the next two years and fourteen matches, Northern Ireland never once found the net. The drought had lasted for over 21 hours of football. Not even David Healy could score and he and his team mates were beginning to wonder if they would ever score again. The team had descended into the abyss – they were becoming the laughing stock of world football.

The best Northern Ireland could do during this goal drought was five goalless draws which included a respectable draw against Spain in 2003. The team's supporters were becoming restless and, when Lawrie Sanchez took over as manager in 2003, a great deal was expected of him. The first expectation was to score a goal and the second to win a match. In his first game in charge, Northern Ireland played Norway at Windsor. The opposition proved far to strong and easily won the match. But, after 56 minutes of the game with Norway already leading 3-0, the unthinkable, the unbelievable and certainly the unexpected happened. Northern Ireland scored a goal.

It was David Healy who ended the agony and scored what was to be just a consolation goal. But the Northern Ireland team had scored and they were treated almost as if they had won the World Cup. Everyone was relieved, from the manager and the team down to the man in the street. They did not have to hold their heads in shame anymore.

Their next two games were against Estonia and Serbia and Montenegro. To everyone's delight Northern Ireland defeated Estonia with David Healy scoring the only goal of the match. They drew against Serbia and Montenegro but the worm had finally turned.

A trip to the Caribbean

In June 2004 the Northern Ireland team set off for a three match tour of the Caribbean. The opposition was not expected to be stiff but it would be a useful training programme for the squad. Depending on the outcome of the matches the chances were that David could pass the Northern Ireland goal record set at 13 goals by Colin Clarke and Billy Gillespie. Leaving Belfast David had already scored ten international goals and four more would put him on the top spot.

The first game, on a very inferior pitch, was against Barbados in Bridgetown and, when the home side went in front and Northern Ireland's Mark Williams had been sent off, it seemed likely that a humiliating defeat was on the cards. However up stepped David Healy to equalise and save his team's blushes. The draw was a poor result but infinitely better than a loss to one of the world's poorest soccer nations. They moved on to the little island of St Kitts where a comfortable 2-0 win restored the side's confidence. Once again David scored one of the goals. His international tally now stood at twelve. He was on the brink of greatness – at least as far as Northern Ireland football was concerned.

On Sunday 6 June 2004, at the Dwight Yorke Stadium in Trinidad, David Healy fulfilled one of his dreams. He hit the back of the net twice in Northern Ireland's 3-0 win over the home side and became the record holder for goals for his country. To have scored this number of goals in his 35 appearances was an impressive achievement. The pundits, including former players like Gerry Armstrong who had turned out 62 times for Northern Ireland and had scored just 12 goals, were predicting at least thirty goals for the young Killyleagh maestro.

David was delighted at his achievement, as were his parents and friends back in Killyleagh, and he was determined to further increase his tally. The statistic, however, which humbled him most was the fact that he had long since beaten the great George Best's tally of nine goals in 38 games for his country.

The greatest goal of all

Back home after the successful tour of the Caribbean Northern Ireland continued with a busy schedule of international matches. By early autumn they had played out a 0-0 draw with Switzerland – making six games without defeat – but were then beaten 3-0 by Poland.

The World Cup qualifier against Wales in Cardiff in September was to become a defining moment in the international career of young David Healy. The game turned out to be one of the most frenetic ever played between the two countries. Early on two players were sent off, one from each side.

Then Northern Ireland went into a 2-0 lead, the second goal being scored by David Healy. In the excitement following the goal, David was booked by the Italian referee and, almost immediately, red-carded for what the referee considered an obscene gesture. The game ended in a 2-2 draw with Northern Ireland finishing the 90 minutes with just nine men. David's display of emotion was fiercely debated in the press for days but the decision stood. David had been sent off for the first time in his international career and would automatically miss the next game. His 38 game run of appearances for his country had been rudely interrupted.

The furore eventually died down. No attempts to persuade the referee to change his decision were successful. In the game against Austria in October Northern Ireland earned a dramatic 3-3 draw although they were defeated in a friendly by Canada and then 4-0 by England in another World Cup qualifier.

But the best had still to come. It had been over thirty years since Northern Ireland had last beaten England and that was at Wembley in 1972 when a Terry Neill goal had broken the long cycle of defeats. Terry Cochrane had scored at Wembley again in 1980 to gain a valuable draw with England in the Home Championships.

But the game which was held at Windsor Park on Wednesday 7 September 2005 was to crown both these previous excellent achievements. England had already beaten Northern Ireland 4-0 at Old Trafford some months earlier. The auguries for Northern Ireland, even in front of an adoring and expectant Belfast crowd, looked bleak. Their team was once again wallowing in the lower positions of the qualifying table.

Northern Ireland 1 – England 0
Windsor Park, Belfast, Wednesday, 7 September 2005
David's 74th minute goal

The 14,000 fans at Windsor that evening, fully realising that Northern Ireland were very much the underdogs, wanted to see a good game and only hoped against hope that perhaps a draw could be achieved. By half time the teams were at stalemate but, as the second half progressed, the home side seemed to be winning most of the play. And then it happened. David Healy received a pinpoint cross from young Steve Davis, swept past the mesmerised defenders and struck the ball into the back of the net past a despairing England keeper. For a split second there was silence and then erupted one of the greatest and loudest cheers ever to have been heard at Windsor Park. In homes throughout the Province and further afield armchair fans jumped off their seats. David Healy had become an instant hero to every man, woman and child in Northern Ireland.

People have been talking about 'the goal' ever since. And yet David's innate modesty prevailed. Although absolutely delighted at his achievement (realising the sensational importance of the goal but actually not considering it his best) he was generous as always and praised his hard working team mates. He simply reminded his ecstatic followers that the win had now to be followed by further success. There were calls for all sorts of recognition for David's feat, like naming football grounds after him. He rather scorned the hysteria and got on with the job in hand – playing for his country.

By the spring of 2006 David had played 46 times for Northern Ireland and had scored nineteen goals. He had always considered how privileged he had been to have travelled to so many lovely and interesting places in the world. He described the Caribbean as 'awesome' and the sights and culture in such cities as Kiev, Prague, Valencia and Sofia, as 'unbelievable'. The future on the international stage was assured for Killyleagh's famous son.

4.
A Continuing League Career

When Preston North End manager, David Moyes, signed David in January 2001 for that impressive £1.5 million, he realised what an asset he had brought to the Deepdale ground. He reckoned that he had uncovered a cut price gem in young Healy. David himself firmly asserted that it was his decision, and his alone, to leave Manchester. In the months that followed Sir Alex Ferguson rued the fact that he had lost such a fine young player although this sentiment sounded rather like sour grapes since he had all but dismissed David as not good enough for his first team by not selecting him.

There were many people who continued to question his decision to leave the mighty Manchester United but David always said that he had done the right thing and that there certainly was life after Old Trafford and Sir Alex Ferguson. Playing at Preston was a refreshing experience especially when it meant finding a regular full time slot in Preston's first team. He became, for a long time, an automatic selection and rarely let his manager down. Playing simultaneously for the Northern Ireland team and for Preston fitted in with David's total commitment to the game. It reminded him of his youth football days when he often played two, if not three, times each Saturday for a number of teams.

For almost four full seasons, David played for the Preston first team on 114 occasions in the league, the FA Cup and the League Cup. He scored 39 times – a goal per match ratio of which any professional footballer would have been justly proud.

In his first season with the club he scored his first professional hat trick against Stockport County although he was disappointed that Preston just missed out on promotion that year losing in a play-off against Bolton Wanderers. But he was decidedly a crowd puller and an extremely popular member of the squad. He was liked and admired both by the fans and by his team mates and, in the 2003/4 season, he was awarded the fans 'Player of the Year' accolade.

Towards the end of his Preston career David went on loan to Norwich City. For a few months in 2003 he enjoyed playing there and made thirteen appearances for the club, scoring two goals. He was annoyed that he did not make the switch permanent. Preston, however, were asking too high a transfer fee for him and so he returned to them early in May 2003.

For another year and a half David continued to play and score for Preston. Newspaper reports, by the autumn of 2004, were rumouring that a move for the young Northern Ireland player seemed imminent. Leeds United were definitely interested in David and it was only after three or four attempts that they finally made an offer which Preston North End were unable to refuse. A transfer fee of around £800,000 was agreed although they were disappointed to lose such a fine and talented player.

David had, by now, completely made up his mind. He had considered, and turned down, Preston's latest contract extension offer for he felt it was time to move. The 30,000 plus crowds at Leeds and the prospect of Premiership professional football were too much of an attraction and he now looked forward to a higher and more challenging level of football. He would need to train hard to ensure first team selection but he was ready and willing to make any sacrifices to become a first team regular at Elland Road.

Football at Leeds United

When David signed for Leeds on 29 October 2004, he immediately made his debut against Wigan at home. They lost 2-0. Three days later, they played Burnley at home. They lost 2-1. He then discovered that his third game would be against his former club, Preston North End. The match at Deepdale just a week after the signing was a mid table clash between two teams whose chances of promotion that season were practically nil. As soon as David came on to the pitch, he was, maybe for the first time in his professional career, roundly booed. There were even those in the Preston crowd who cried 'Judas' when David appeared in his new team strip. But this did not faze David – he knew he would have a cool reception and just accepted the home crowd's obvious displeasure.

The faces of that same home crowd were then ground into the dirt when their erstwhile protégé, young Mr Healy, proceeded to score – not once but twice. Leeds easily won the game 4-2. It was a baptism of fire for David. He had been taken very quickly to the hearts of the Elland Road faithful.

As the games went on, Leeds had their fair share of victories but there were disappointments as well. David, however, was regularly finding the net and keeping up Leeds' faint hopes of promotion. But it was not to be in that season. At the commencement of the 2005/6 year David was being quoted in the local and national press that he was confident of helping Leeds to gain promotion. This was not just idle bombast – he knew his capabilities and he was determined to work extra hard to make a great contribution which, if his team mates also pulled their weight, could make the difference between having a good season and having a great one.

The management at Leeds was ambitious for the club and they had great expectations too. In the 2005/6 season, between August 2005 and April 2006, Leeds won 19 games, drew 16 and lost 5 and David scored 16 goals. However in the same period he was yellow carded six times and sent off against Queen's Park Rangers on 17 September 2005, just ten days after his glory goal against England. The manager continued to select David although there were some games when he just came on as a substitute.

David enjoys football at Leeds. He realises that he must fight for his place in the team but feels that he has already made a valuable contribution to help their chances of promotion to the Premiership although, unfortunately, the team just missed out yet again. He loves playing in front of huge crowds and revels in the cut and thrust of senior English football at the highest level. He sees his career with the club continuing for the foreseeable future and, provided he can continue to score goals, his time at Leeds appears secure.

5.
Life beyond Football

Throughout the past years David has been the recipient of many awards. In his younger days he returned home with every type of cup and shield when playing in junior football. His mother originally paid him 50p for every goal he scored. It must have seemed a good idea at the time for Irene would have wanted to show her encouragement for her football-crazy son. But when he came home telling her that he had scored perhaps 10 goals in one day and often over 100 in a season, she had to change her plans. A word of congratulation would have to suffice in the future.

David's photograph has continued to be a regular feature in every class of newspaper and journal. There is no argument that, in Northern Ireland at least, his is one of the best known faces in the field of sport and beyond. In 2000 he won the Belfast Telegraph Sports BBC Award and it was his father who picked up the accolade from George Best that night as David could not be present.

Sports award ceremonies have become an integral part of David's life. He is almost as well known in his black tie and evening suit as he is in his football strip. In 2004, after becoming the Northern Ireland record scorer, he was presented with the *Belfast Telegraph* Sports Star of the Year award. This accomplishment was repeated the next year when he was the first sportsperson to win the same award back to back. This time he easily beat off all possible challengers for that honour after 'that goal' against England in September. In the audience that same evening was Calum Best who handed over the George Best Breakthrough Award for the first time. The recipient was David's Northern Ireland team mate, Steve Davis, whose precision pass to David had resulted in the goal that defeated England. This was a popular choice.

David never seeks the limelight when he helps at charity events and when he lends his name to good and just causes. Being a modest young man he believes that it is his duty to assist when he can. He returns to Killyleagh often to join his former colleagues at Killyleagh Youth Club commemorative events. He remembers those who gave him help in his early days.

In June 2006 a mural was unveiled in Killyleagh depicting the town's three international players – Hugh Henry Davey who played in the 1920s and who actually captained Ireland on at least one occasion; Terry Cochrane who played and scored in the 1970s and 1980s and David Healy himself. It is a fitting tribute to the marvellous achievements of these three talented international footballers.

Family and friends

David's greatest and most faithful supporters have always been his parents, Clifford and Irene. They have encouraged him; they have given him every possible opening and they have kept his feet firmly on the ground. David's modesty and courtesy have come from his early days at home in Killyleagh. Although football was the top priority, he has found time to participate in other activities in the town – at Beavers, at the Boys Brigade, at the church and at every event run by his school and local football clubs. He is truly a son of Killyleagh for, no matter that he has become a star and hero in the wider soccer scene, he has remembered his roots. That is what makes the young man such a favourite.

Clifford, Irene, and, of course, David's great friend and confidant, Maurice Garrett, have made lots of sacrifices – from the simplest, such as the regular lifts to the Olympia Centre in Belfast and the continual washing of football kit; to the greatest, like the preparations for the next schoolboy international match and the final farewell from Killyleagh when he moved to live in England. Anyone who knows the commitment of Irene and Clifford will agree that David has been more than fortunate with the love and care he has received from such wonderful parents. At home, too, he has always been able to count on the support of his sister, Lana, and his brother, Clifford.

David is married to Emma and they have two children, Taylor Jane, who is five years old, and Jude David who was born in the summer of 2005. Little Taylor loves watching her daddy on television but usually gets him mixed up with that other fairly notable footballer, David Beckham.

He has lived in Manchester for some years now and this will be the family's home in the foreseeable future. He has made many friends there and feels as settled as any Killyleagh man can be when exiled from his native Northern Ireland. Visits home to county Down are made as often as time permits and he certainly always looks forward to being back in Killyleagh amongst the friends of his childhood.

David has kept up with many of his football colleagues and friends. He is close to people like Damien Johnson who played with him at every level for Northern Ireland. Keith Gillespie, Roy Carroll and Andrew Smith are firm friends and he has known them since his early days playing for Lisburn Youth football.

There is one very important aspect in a professional footballer's life. If he is free from injury then his career can go from strength to strength. If he succumbs to niggling injuries then his game is often blighted. As far as David Healy is concerned, he has remained remarkably clear of hurt and harm in the game. He has suffered occasionally from slight injuries but none of these have kept him out of the game for long. Training regularly and maintaining a wise regimen in life, which he has always done, will surely keep him playing the game for years to come.

Having a strict lifestyle is important to David. He realises that he must keep healthy and this he is determined to do. He does have ambitions after he finally hangs up his football boots. He is keen to remain involved in the game which has, after all, given him so many opportunities and openings from his earliest years. He is interested in becoming a coach and has the greatest ambition of all for a Northern Ireland international – and that is, at some time in the future, to manage the national side. People in Killyleagh could think of no better man to do this worthwhile job – but they are biased. Time will tell.

Like all good parents he wants to spend more time with his growing children and, like so many retired footballers, he wants to play more golf. He took up the game when he was still living at home. He joined Ringdufferin Golf Club where he was then considered to be a fine player. His options, therefore, are wide open. For David Healy, however, there is one certain goal in life. It is the goal he has always had in his years thus far – and that is to continue to fill every hour with every aspect of sport, whether playing it, managing it or sharing his considerable skills with the young people of the future.

Killyleagh may not seem a particularly big or important place on the map but, as we can see yet again, this time in the guise of David Healy, it has continued to produce remarkable people who have contributed not only to its own town but also to Northern Ireland as a whole. Killyleagh is indeed the envy of many of its neighbours. It can carry on basking in the glory of its famous sons – including its most recent one, the outstanding and talented David Healy.

David depicted on the Killyleagh mural

Notes and References

Sir Hans Sloane

1. McGregor, Arthur (ed), *Sir Hans Sloane – Collector, Scientist, Antiquary* (London 1994) p.12.
2. Brooks, E. St. John, *Sir Hans Sloane, the Great Collector and his Circle* (London 1954) p.51.
3. Ibid. p.155.
4. de Beer, G.R., *Sir Hans Sloane and the British Museum* (Oxford) p.152.

Sir Henry Blackwood

1. Masefield, John, *Sea Life in Nelson's Time* (London 1905) p.66.
2. Bennett, Leslie H., *Nelson's Eyes – the Life and Correspondence of Vice Admiral Sir Henry Blackwood KCB* (Brussels 2005) p. 13.
3. Ibid. pp. 107/8.
4. Ibid. p.63.
5. Ibid. p.86.
6. Ibid. p.97.
7. Ibid. p.99.
8. Ibid. p.180.
9. Ibid. p.193.
10. Ulster Architectural Heritage Society, *Clandeboye* (Belfast 1985) p.37.

Dr Henry Cooke

1. McCreery, Alexander, *The Presbyterian Ministers of Killileagh* (Belfast 1885) p.232.
2. Holmes, Finlay, *Our Irish Presbyterian Heritage* (Belfast 1985) p. 100.
3. McCreery, Alexander, *The Presbyterian Ministers of Killileagh* (Belfast 1885) p. 271.

Dr Edward Hincks

1. Davidson, E.F., *Edward Hincks – a Selection from his Correspondence with a Memoir* (Oxford 1933) p.90.
2. Ibid. p.22.
3. Ibid. p.56.
4. Ibid. p.54.
5. Ibid. p.73.
6. Ibid. p.64.

Bibliography

Henry Blackwood
1. Bennett, Leslie H., *Nelson's Eyes – the Life and Correspondence of Vice Admiral Sir Henry Blackwood KCB*, Brussels, 2005.
2. Fitchett, W.H., *Nelson and his Captains*, London, 1902.
3. Masefield, John, *Sea Life in Nelson's Time*, London, 1905.
4. Oman, Carola, *Nelson*, London, 1950.
5. Ulster Architectural Heritage Society (Ulster House Series), *Clandeboye*, Belfast, 1985.
6. Ulster Architectural Heritage Society (reprinted from Country Life), *Killyleagh Castle*, Belfast, 1970.
7. White, Colin and the 1805 Club, *The Trafalgar Captains – their Lives and Memorials*, London, 2005.

Sir Hans Sloane
1. de Beer, G.R., *Sir Hans Sloane and the British Museum*, Oxford, 1953.
2. Brooks, E. St. John, *Sir Hans Sloane – the Great Collector and his Circle*, London, 1954.
3. McGregor, Arthur (ed), *Sir Hans Sloane – Collector, Scientist, Antiquary*, London, 1994.

Dr Edward Hincks
1. Cathcart, Kevin J., *The Edward Hincks Bicentenary*, Dublin, 1994.
2. Davidson, E.F., *Edward Hincks – a Selection from his Correspondence with a Memoir*, Oxford, 1933.

Henry Cooke
1. Holmes, Finlay, *Our Irish Presbyterian Heritage*, Belfast, 1985.
2. McCreery, Alexander, *The Presbyterian Ministers of Killileagh*, Belfast, 1885.
3. Porter, J.L., *The Life and Times of Henry Cooke*, Dublin, 1871.

Terry Cochrane and David Healy
1. Brodie, Malcolm and Kennedy, Billy (eds), *The Irish Football Association – 125 Years, the History*, Belfast, 2005.
2. Hayes, Dean, *Northern Ireland's Greats – 100 Top Football Heroes*, Belfast 2005.